Early Closing Day

Air Raids on Reading 1939 –1945

Mike Cooper

Scallop Shell Press

Cover design © John R Mullaney FSAI
http://www.thetopdraw.com

First published 2016

ISBN 978-0-9935512-1-5

Published by Scallop Shell Press

29 Derby Road,

Caversham,

Reading.

RG4 5HE

Contents

Early Closing Day

> To honour the memory
>
> of those
>
> who lost their lives
>
> as a result of the bombs
>
> that fell in this area
>
> on
>
> 10 February 1943

Memorial plaque on the wall of the offices of Blandy and Blandy's solicitors next to St. Laurence's Church, Reading.

Introduction

This study began as part of preparation to teach a course on war and society in Reading for the Worker's Education Association, and grew through preparation for a series of talks for Reading Libraries and other local groups.

It is an attempt to document, and provide a general context for, all known air raids on Reading during the Second World War. For this purpose "Reading" has been defined as the then Borough, with areas of Tilehurst, Earley and particularly Woodley, which were not then included.

Chapter 1 looks at Reading's preparedness for bombing – Civil Defence, air raid shelters and the organisation behind this. Chapters 2 and 3 look at the actual air raids themselves, with Chapter 3 concentrating on a detailed picture of the events of the 10th February 1943 – the "Peoples' Pantry" raid - using official primary sources. The final chapters look at the immediate aftermath of the 1943 raid and how it has been remembered.

One colleague at Reading Reference Library, as it then was, described me as a "fun free zone" when it came to writing history – well, I hope it was just when it came to writing history. This is not an account of life in Reading in World War Two, and my approach is to look at organisations, and what can be said from official sources created at the time. As a result, I have used contemporary newspaper material, and particularly the growing body of oral history, only sparingly.

Part of the justification for this lies in the availability of this material elsewhere – Stuart Hylton's fine books, the work done by the Friends of HistoryPin and the BBC to collect and record people's memories of their lives in wartime Reading. However, another part, perhaps the greater one, has its roots in my experience of telling the story of bombing in Reading.

Oral history is a powerful source of impression, colour and incident. It has been used in local and national history to reach topics hidden in the official record, and at best it is vivid and moving. In the case of Reading many people in their seventies, and beyond, recall bombs dropping, broken glass and narrow escapes, but these accounts have to be treated with caution. Memory, subsequent experience, reading about the subject and the very real pleasure of talking and being listened to, can all distort the record given. It should not be forgotten that there are things about, let us say, the People's Pantry raid that a ten year old eye witness could not be expected to know at the time.

Early Closing Day

I have purposely avoided using some of the recurring stories told to me: the German pilot who deliberately missed Woodley airfield as he had flown from there before the war; the spy and the BBC transmitter in the People's Pantry and the fact that Vincent's was the target that day. I have found no contemporary evidence to support any of these. This does not mean that they aren't true, but that in the absence of any corroboration from a wartime source, they have had to give way to things I can support.

By 2016, I had given perhaps a dozen talks about air raids on Reading to a variety of audiences and I had started to hear from witnesses or relatives of witnesses things I have said told as a contemporary account. Again, without an actual wartime account, I'm wary of using such material, although I acknowledge fully that it represents one facet of Reading's experience of bombing in WW2.

There is room for a study of WW2 and popular memory in Reading.

A vivid collection of interviews and press cuttings was assembled under the title *Terror Raid Reading* and is held in a ring binder dated February 2013 in Reading Local Studies Library. This appears to be the working notes from Colin Drury who was working on a book of the same name. As far as I can tell this was never published.

The local press featured attacks on Reading, but censorship and self censorship meant that details were seldom given, and the tenor was such as to either play down what had happened, or highlight aspects for propaganda. I'm fortunate that Stuart Hylton has grappled with this!

Photographs from the collection held at Reading Local Studies Library have been used here. The other major resource of relevance is the *Berkshire Chronicle* collection held by Reading Museum. There is almost certainly a photo-history of Reading in WW2 waiting to be done!

The main primary sources used here are the minutes of the Civil Defence Committee and the logs of incidents and other reports made by the Head Warden. Reading itself has a strikingly complete set, but this set stops at the Borough Boundary, so that frustratingly, a given "stick" of bombs may be documented so far and then no further. The accounts are simple statements of what happened, and are not reflections in most cases. They cannot always be used to ascertain if a given set of actions were correct, or if better alternatives existed. They also represent only one aspect of the picture, and are devoid of any direct evidence of individual experiences. This means that this is very much a bureaucratic history.

My only access to the German side of these events has been through secondary sources or their republishing of primary sources. This means that a key dimension has been neglected, as is the case with Allied forces records. One consequence of this has been a limit to my ability to talk about anti-aircraft defence and the activities of the Home Guard. Similarly, I must acknowledge that more work is needed on the role of the police and fire service in civil defence in Reading.

Secondary sources have been used chiefly for matters of detail – such as the characteristics of a particular bomber – or general policy.

I've chosen to cite my sources in endnotes for each chapter, with general items used in a separate bibliography. There are a number of reasons for this. Firstly, I find I need to know why I know something, and so have to keep a record of where I found it. Secondly, whilst it may clutter the page this means that anyone who wants to use this book in their own research can follow in my tracks. Thirdly, and perhaps less pragmatically, the failure of a disturbingly wide range of local history books about Reading to give usable references, makes me cross and frustrated when I try to use them myself. Finally, the bombing raids on Reading have entered our collective memory to a degree that some things are becoming "facts" that aren't – I feel it important to distinguish what is a matter of record and what a matter of memory, rumour or speculation.

Perhaps, if *Early Closing Day* does turn out to be a "fun free zone", it is because my own experience of what was happening through the sources used has shown me a picture of a time that could be fun, but, when Reading was grimly organised to deal with a potentially deadly and devastating threat.

Acknowledgements

All sorts of people gave all sorts of help and encouragement during this project – which I see from my footnotes is now in its fourth or fifth year. Colleagues at the Berkshire Record Office, Reading Library and Reading Museum gave invaluable professional support. In particular I'd like to thank Ann Smith and Katie Amos of the Local Studies Library (I'm biased, but I think it's the finest resource for Berkshire history around, and colleagues' standards of knowledge, helpfulness and flexibility are un-matched) and Brendan Carr of Reading Museum. Staff at the National Archives, RVS archive and Historic England library all gave access to material that helped turn corners.

John Mullaney and Scallop Shell Press have been wonderful to work with at a business and personal level.

Early Closing Day

Margaret Simons helped show me that I could still "do history" and that "local history" need not be a collection of "twee jottings". Amanda Holland gave boundless enthusiasm, practical help and good counsel during a hectic round of talks. Mike Bond, Bob Hall, Richard Marks and Neil Grant all tolerated me burbling away incessantly about ARP and incendiaries and gave great practical and morale (and moral) help. Rebecca Pentland shared her own work, historical good sense and what, in another context, would be an rather odd fascination with the doings of Air Raid Wardens (it is possible to get excited by finding that last British Restaurant). John Whithead did me a huge favour by lending me copies of the Civil Defence Committee minutes and proofs for his Reading buses book. Nicci Shepherd and Michele Spiller volunteered to proof read the text.

A very great number of other people contributed in all sorts of ways, and a lot of them are mentioned in the text. Many more - not least the members of the Old Reading group on Facebook – offered memories, "Oooh, what a good idea" and "I think that was at such and such". At almost every talk I've given, someone told me something useful, stimulating or moving, and I'd like to thank you all.

Finally, at home, Miriam (who married me despite this book) and Dave the Cat (well maybe not so much Dave, but...) understood, encouraged, helped and hugged someone who has tended to react to the mention of any street in Reading by saying "Oh, that was bombed in nineteen-wotsit..." and smiled whilst doing so.

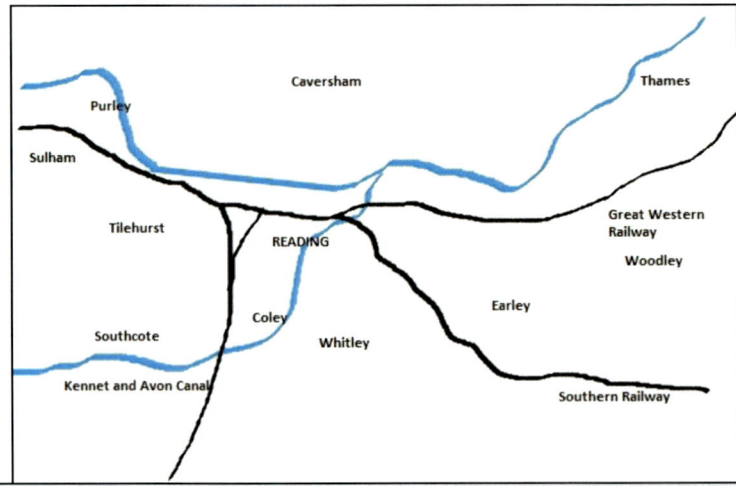

Reading Area, c.1940, showing places mentioned in the text

Chronology of Air Raids on the Reading Area 1940-44

1940

Aug	16th	Woodley
Sept	11th/12th	Woodley
	12th	Reading Gasworks
	16th	Woodley
	30th	Erleigh Court and Suttons Seeds
Oct	1st	Caversham
	3rd	Woodley
	5th	Coley
	6th	Woodley
	9th	Caversham
	11th/12th	Earley
Nov	5th	Tilehurst/Sulham
	15th	Coley Park Farm
	26th	Caversham/Reading
Dec	1st/2nd	Earley

1941

Jan	26th	Caversham
	30th	Woodley
April	9th	Tilehurst Rd/Berkeley Ave
May	10th	Suttons Seeds
	12th	Gasworks machine gunned

1942

June	21st/22nd	Woodley

1943

Feb	10th	Four bombs on the centre of Reading, machine gunning in Caversham, Broad St, Stone St, Oxford Rd. Tilehurst

1944

June	19th	Flying Bomb on Earley

Early Closing Day

Images of actual bomb damage in Reading are rare, and those showing Civil Defence at work in wartime rarer still. These two photographs show exercises run before the War, on 28th February and 10th August 1939, but give an impression of the work undertaken and the equipment used. The August 1939 exercise tested "E Group" in the area around Coley, where it is believed that this photograph was taken. The February photograph was taken in Berkeley Avenue. The Rescue Parties in the both images seem to be wearing anti-gas suits to protect against mustard gas. Both come from the *Berkshire Chronicle*, and were published on the 3rd March and the 18th August 1939.

Chapter 1
Preparing to be Bombed

The Target

In 1939 around 100,000 people lived in Reading. At the last census – 1931 – there had been just over 97,000 and at that point the Town's population had risen by 16,000 in the past ten years.

The look of the town, and its extent, was still very much a product of expansion after the arrival of the railways in the 1840s, and especially from the 1870s. Red brick houses, most using local bricks and tiles from Tilehurst, had pushed along the Oxford Road, linked the town to the Caversham Bridge and reached into Katesgrove and Whitley in the South. In the East, Reading itself stopped beyond Palmer Park, blurring into Earley. Woodley as still very much a separate entity.

Before the arrival of the Inner Distribution Road, and development in the early 1970s around what was until only recently the Civic Centre, housing reached up to St Mary's Butts, along the now lost streets such as Hope Street and Soho Street. Following the first council house building on the Shinfield Road, Whitley itself had just seen a major period of council house building, starting in 1929 that added around 2000 homes to the Borough – two thirds of all council building in the periods. By the start of World War Two, 11% of Reading's population lived in a Council home.[1]

Tilehurst was still largely rural. Although housing was being built in what would now be called "Old Norcot", the area's main period of development, like that in Southcote, would come after the War. Much of what is now viewed as Coley and most of Southcote were "green" – south of the Bath Road buses went no further than Berkeley Avenue.

Caversham, like Tilehurst, joined the Borough in 1911, but had also yet to see the expansion that took it to its present shape, although it was spreading uphill towards Emmer Green, and along and around the Henley Road.

Reading made its living on manufacturing, with the "3Bs" – biscuits, beer and bulbs – still major employers. The 1939 Kelly's Directory for the town said *[Reading's] chief business is to be found in biscuit making, iron foundries and engine works and seed growing, malting and brewing*

A quick look at Census data and at a map from the time would add *and railways* - the Southern Railway and the Great Western Railway (GWR) both had stations, with a major GWR junction at Reading West. The railways provided jobs for 1800 people from a workforce of around 32-33,000 in 1931. Over 5000 worked in baking of some form, with Huntley and Palmers probably the largest single

Early Closing Day

employer, although the firm, like many in the town suffered in the inter-war depression.

Throughout this book costs and wages are given in contemporary figures with no attempt to adjust to 2016 levels. In 1940 the national average male weekly wage in manufacturing was 89 shillings - £4 9s.   A woman would earn 38/11 – 38 shillings and 11 pence (also written as 38s 11d). Men worked an average 48hour week.[2]

German aerial photo of Reading, summer 1940. Part of a small sequence showing the area, which was accompanied by a map giving general navigation points. On this photograph, taken from about 10,000 feet, the rivers and railway show up clearly. "A", just right of centre is the junction at Reading West. "e" at the left is the airfield at Woodley. (© Colopix historical images)

The manufacturing base gave rise to a strong Labour movement – with the "Co-op" an important part of the town, and the town had had its first woman Mayor, Edith Sutton in 1933. However, in 1939 the Corporation was run by a Liberal-Conservative coalition supporting Neville Chamberlain's National Government.

Although present, neither of the two most sharply contesting ideologies of the 1930s – fascism and communism – had made much impact in Reading, despite an active Communist Party.

Brock Barracks, on the Oxford Road, was the Depot for the Royal Berkshire Regiment, although in 1939 the 2nd Battalion was in India. The 1st Battalion would join the British Expeditionary Force in France on the outbreak of war. There were also territorial units based in and around Reading. As in the rest of the UK, conscription began to be introduced on April 1939 and would be expanded later.

Rationing arrived at the start of 1940, although food price controls had been introduced just before the war. During WW2 Reading would see a range of specific was related industry - Spitfire fuselages were made by Vincent's in town, for example - and on the Thames, Elliott's would build landing craft. In Woodley, Phillips and Powis built training aircraft under the Miles name, after Fred Miles their talented designer.

Expectations

On September 1st 1939, the Reading Corporation's Emergency Committee for Civil Defence held its first meeting. After agreeing to meet every day at 10am, the Committee's first item of business were telegrams from the Home Office directing the carrying out of certain of the provisional local war instructions.[3]

The instructions had been issued in March 1939.

When war was declared – even when war appeared inevitable - it was generally believed that Reading would be bombed. The town's preparations for this provided a thread in the everyday life of all its inhabitants and consumed considerable resources and effort. An understanding of what was intended and provided is important to any picture of how Reading reacted when it was attacked.

The common understanding amongst planners in the late 1930s was that the next war would see sudden, large scale and utterly catastrophic air raids on Britain. These would be impossible to stop, would probably involve poison gas, and would cause heavy loss of life, homelessness and displacement of people. In 1939 it was forecast that that the German bomber force could drop 700 tons of bombs per day over the first two weeks of a war.[4] Five years earlier, as Britain began working up its preparations for attack, an official report suggested 150,000 casualties in a week.[5]

At one stage by 1942 the area around Reading had provision for feeding and temporary shelter for 120,000 people.[6]

To a certain extent this conviction was based on prophesy and theory, but those calling for a high level of national civil defence could point to attacks on Madrid, Barcelona and Guernica, amongst others during Germany's intervention in the Spanish Civil War, and the inclusion of hundreds of bombers in German rearmament.

Reading had not been bombed in the Great War, and only the handful of

Early Closing Day

Reading people who had volunteered to serve the Republican cause in Spain had any direct experience of modern air attack.[7]

The town would receive evacuees from London – both on a centrally organised scale and at an individual level – but there is no sign in the records that evacuation was seriously considered for Reading itself.

Hindsight shows that the Luftwaffe, the German Air Force, did not have the capacity to deliver such raids, and despite heavy bombing of London, Coventry and cities from Southampton – where Reading fire crews served – to Belfast, nothing matched even the scale of attack delivered by the RAF and USAAF against Germany.

Reading's precautions against air attack need to be seen against this background, and with relatively few air attacks, the town's experience of "ARP" would be more of these precautions than their actual use.

With the advance of Allied armies after D-Day (June 1944), and with it the reduction of the threat of bombing, the whole Civil Defence infrastructure of the United Kingdom began to be dismantled during the second half of 1944. Reading received the Ministry of Home Security's "Circular 47/1945" formally disbanding the wartime Civil Defence organisation on 4th May 1945.

This chapter will concentrate on the period up to 1943, and the last full air attack on the town.[8]

The survival of the Corporation's committee minutes covering Civil Defence means that a very detailed picture of how Reading was organised for defence against air attack is available, and what is given here is a general outline only, with the intention of identifying key services and provision. By contrast, without further research some services such as Police and Fire can only be sketched in.

Organising

Originally known as "Air Raid Precautions" (ARP) – and often thought of as such today – the organisations responsible for the civilian response to air attack, were more widely known as "Civil Defence" (CD), and in 1941 the ARP arm was renamed Civil Defence. Technically ARP had always been part of the overall picture of Civil Defence, which extended to fires and police services. The two terms will be used alongside one another as most discussion will be of the situation in Reading in 1940-41.

The basic framework for all this had been put in place by two Acts of Parliament

– the Air Raids Precautions Act of 1937, and the Civil Defence Act of 1939. By the middle of the Second World War over 800,000 people in Britain were directly involved in ARP work.[9]

Wardens at post C5, Grovelands, 1938.
Dating to before the clinic was built on this site in 1939/40, this shows the team at post C5 at around the time of the Munich Crisis, or shortly after. Their appearance – only respirators and military style steel helmets have been issued to them – would be quite representative of the first couple of years of the War too. At left, the teenager is probably the one of the Post's Boy Scout messengers. In the centre of the rear row is Mr. W. Willett, who was Borough Architect at the time.
(Reading Libraries 1254303)

There were two main roles for Civil Defence in Reading inWW2:

1. Actual defence against bombs

2. Responding to the effects of raids

After looking at the structure behind this, this chapter will look at the various branches of civil defence in turn under these headings.

Reading formed part of Air Raid Precautions Region 6, whose headquarters were at Marlborough House in Parkside Road.[10]

Berkshire itself was divided into four "Warning Areas" for air raid warnings, with Reading falling in its own area, covering at first most of the east of Berkshire, and later most of the County other than the far west and north.[11]

The Regional Commissioner – in 1942 Sir Harry Haig - presided over team drawn from the military, national and local government covering functions including

Early Closing Day

Wardens, September 1944.
Dressed in the issue blue Civil Defence uniform of the time – contrasting with the wardens at Grovelands in the previous photograph - these are Wardens from the headquarters of "F" Group, covering the area between Katesgrove and Christchurch Road. They would probably have been based in Kendrick Road.
The caption from Reading Libraries identifies them as: On the back row: Roberts (Deputy Head Warden); Adams (Deputy Head Warden); Percival (Warden); Osborne (Deputy Head Warden). Middle row, seated: Stenning (Warden); Wasley (Warden); Roberts (Head Warden); Goodey (Warden). At the front, seated on the ground, is Ranwell (messenger).   (Reading Libraries 1291362)

Map of Oxford Road area 1940 showing the location of Civil Defence posts and shelters.As this detailed view shows, Wardens' Posts are marked "W",
First aid posts "+" and public air raid shelters with a triangle and a number showing their capacity – 100 would mean a shelter for 100 people.
(Reading Museum).

transport, information, feeding and reconstruction. Haig reported upwards to the Home Office, ultimately to the Home Secretary.

Locally, Air Raid Precautions were undertaken by local government – in the documentary record, this is marked by a split in coverage between Berkshire and Reading, then a County Borough. The County's own Civil Defence services had their Headquarters in Shire Hall in Reading, although direct communication between the two is only mentioned occasionally by either organisation.

The Local Authority was expected to provide for "Homelessness, evacuation, re-housing, first aid repairs, disposal of dead, sewers, casualty services, feeding, decontamination and Civil defence."[12] Local authorities were also to plan "mutual aid" with neighbours – Berkshire County Council made provision for its Rest Centres in the North of the County to be used by Oxford.[13]

In the Borough ARP was coordinated by the Civil Defence Emergency Committee – also referred to as the Emergency Committee for Civil Defence, and later the Emergency and Invasion Committee. This was chaired by the Mayor and covered the Wardens' Service, Casualty Service, Rescue, Decontamination, and Fire. Responsibility ranged from the supply of shelters, to information and advice.

The last minuted meeting of the Committee was under Cllr. Phoebe Cusden in 1947. Local authority provision was supplemented by a range of regionally and nationally provided services.

Report and Control Centre

The Centre was expected to be the hub of the civil defence effort in the town, coordinating medical efforts, life saving, measures against poison gas and repair and rescue. It was linked with the ARP headquarters and with regional support. The Centre was based in the "supper room and adjoining room" of the Town Hall and was staffed "day and night".[15]

In July 1940, the Borough reported that the Centre was staffed by 12 men and 36 women with 30 male messengers.[16]

Civil Defence Emergency Committee, 1940[14]
Major Cllr. W.E.C McIllroy
Alderman W.H.. Bale
Alderman A. Lovell
Cllr J.E. Edmonson
ARP Officer Cmdr. J. Hassard-Short RN. (Retd.)
Equipment Officer Mr. E.R.W Gillmor

Early Closing Day

Adult male staff were paid £3 per week, female staff £2 - the messengers were Boy Scouts supervised by a Mr F. W. Jennings.[17] The initial intention had been to employ solely female staff, but within a matter of days of the outbreak of war the Town Clerk reported that he had been unable to find enough women workers.[18] Sleeping accommodation for night staff was provided in the Small Town Hall – eight beds were authorised by the Civil Defence Committee on 1st November 1939 - and *The comfort of the staff [...] provided for by rest rooms, games, cinematograph and canteen.*[19]

Boy Scouts, used as messengers, were provided with nine bunks in the Town Hall basement.[20] Key staff – the Mayor, controller and others were provided with - *sleeping accommodation and breakfast in [32] Market Place* [21] at a cost of £140 a year. The building was later described as a "Victory Hostel"

Back up provision was discussed, initially at Sidmouth House, but then centres were developed in Caversham and Whitley. That at 12 Priest Hill was first mentioned in Committee minutes in August 1941. In July that year approval was given for conversion of a building at Whitley Rise. Costing between £1500 and £1600 at the time, two-thirds of the cost of the Centre, which was to be equipped with six telephones was to be borne by the Ministry of Home Security.[22]

By May 1942, the Civil Defence Committee was being briefed on the need to staff the Town Hall and Caversham centres during the day, with night time cover at Caversham and Whitley.[23] The fact that eight staff were needed for Caversham, as opposed to three at each of the other centres reflects the round the clock cover involved, and also hints at a shift of emphasis recognising night as opposed to day raids as the main threat. Ironically, the Town Hall centre would be knocked out during a daylight attack in 1943.

Defence against attack

The defences prepared to protect Reading against air attack took two main forms

1. Active – anti aircraft guns, for example

2. Passive – warnings and shelters.

This section will concentrate on Civil defence measures, but first it will give a very brief description of the active measures taken in WW2.

Defending the town [24]

The ultimate defence of Reading against air attack rested with RAF Fighter Command (later Air Defence of Great Britain) and the Army, with the latter manning searchlights, sound location and anti-aircraft guns.

The immediate anti-aircraft defence of Reading involved three main elements —

A. Anti aircraft guns   B. Searchlights   C. Bombing decoys

Anti Aircraft Guns

Anti aircraft - "AA" or "Ack-Ack" - guns were intended either to shoot down bombing aircraft, or much more likely, force them to break up their formations, bomb from an unfavourable altitude or, ultimately, go somewhere else. Performance, in terms of aircraft shot down, was poor for all nations' guns throughout most of the Second World War. At the start of the Blitz, the British calculated that they needed to fire 6000 shells to be even reasonably sure of a hit.[25]

"Vulnerable Points" (VPs) would be defended by light anti aircraft guns — typically, (although by no means always, especially in 1939-40 — the 40mm Bofors gun. If the defence provided for Miles factory in Swindon was mirrored at Woodley, then the Miles works — VP 545 - would have had a single Bofors gun providing local defence against fast low level attack.

Heavy anti aircraft guns — in most cases the excellent 3.7 inch — were used to tackle higher flying targets, and a battery of guns based near Reading might actually be part of a wider system of anti aircraft defences.

In 1939-40 Reading was part of the Basingstoke Gun Defended Area, and was the responsibility of 5th Anti Aircraft Division, Royal Artillery with its headquarters in Reading. The Royal Artillery's "AA Command" of which 5th AA Division was part, reported to RAF Fighter Command. Initially manned by the Territorial Army, manning anti-aircraft batteries eventually, and controversially, passed to the Home Guard. Women soldiers of the Auxiliary Territorial Service (ATS) were used to operate equipment such as rangefinders and to operate searchlights.

The town itself was not a first order priority for anti-aircraft defence, but by 1942, 5 AA Division deployed a single battery in two half-batteries of four 3.7inch guns around Reading. The location names given are those quoted in the 1942 source, additional details are from published Ordnance Survey references and are only approximate.

Early Closing Day

BY3   Tanners Farm – north of Gravel Hill in Emmer Green.

BY5   Toutley – In Earley, just south of what is now the A329M/M4 Junction

In addition to these, hard standings for guns had been prepared at

BY1   Amners Farm – Just south of what is now the M4 and east of the Burghfield Road.

BY2   Tilehurst – probably in McIlroy Park

BY4   Sonning – south of the Bath Road

BY6   Crocker's Farm – Earley, south of what is now Chatteris Way

The site at Tanners Farm had its own gun laying radar.

Not present in any of the published records are the "Z battery" remembered as being in Whitley, and a gun (or guns) which are remembered as standing on the roundabout at the junction of Hartland Road and Northumberland Avenue.

Memories are not precise, and the "gun" and the Z launchers may have been one and the same – at least one account recalls a multi barrelled gun, which can almost certainly only have been a Z "Projector".

A "Z" Battery was a group of rocket launchers firing a mass of unguided projectiles at any attacker, and relying on sheer numbers of rockets in the air for a hit. There was an army camp, later used as a prisoner of war camp, off Northumberland Avenue where the South Reading Leisure Centre now stands.

Without a more detailed check on individual battery records, it's not possible to confirm if and when any of the guns (or rockets) engaged German aircraft, although, in May 1943, the Emergency and Invasion Committee of the Corporation heard of arrangements to warn the public about any exercises by Home Guard batteries and Berkshire had a Home Guard manned Z Battery with enrolment beginning in May 1942.[27]

Searchlights

Searchlights, controlled at first from sound locators, but later by RADAR, either worked hand in hand with guns, or, early on in the war could be used to direct night fighters onto German bombers. Although at first they were the responsibility of the Royal Engineers, for most of the war searchlight batteries were manned by the Royal Artillery.

342 Searchlight Battery, 35 Searchlight Regiment, Royal Artillery had its Headquarters in the Village Hall at Woodcote, and operated from six positions around Reading, each probably comprising a single light:

Position	Location
508 31	Sulham – actually west of Long Lane, not far from where Denefield School is now
508 32	Coldharbour Farm in Cray's Pond
508 33	Cane End – between Cane End and Gallowstree Common
508 34	Crowsley Farm – north of Devil's Hill, near Sonning Common
508 35	West of St Peter's Avenue, Caversham Heights
508 36	South of the Burghfield Road, near the Cunning Man pub.

341 Searchlight Battery based in Hurley operated a position just to the north of Sonning with another at Crockers Farm, Earley probably associated with the Heavy Anti Aircraft position there.

Decoys

Work to create decoys to draw German bombers away from city targets began in summer 1940. However, following the attack on Coventry in November 1940, where a successful concentration of incendiary bombs had started fires which guided following waves of bombers to the target, decoy sites – know as 'Special Fire', or more popularly, "Starfish" sites - were set up around significant targets.

Manned by RAF Barrage Balloon Command, these varied in sophistication, but in general comprised purpose built oil and waste fed burners to create the impression of a target under attack, so drawing off German aircraft. Reading eventually had three such sites:

SF29a – Binfield - between Binfield and Shurlock Row

SF29b – Arborfield – to the north of Arborfield itself

SF29c – Sulham – between Sulham and where the M4 is now

The Reading decoys were scheduled to be decommissioned from 1944. Although it may be tempting to explain the bombing of Binfield and Arborfield by reference to the decoys, they were to be used only after the first wave of bombers had hit the target, and, for example, the bombs that fell on Sulham in November 1940 almost certainly fell before the Starfish site was in place.

Early Closing Day

Defending the people

The immediate physical defence for the people of Reading was the responsibility of the Corporation and was provided by

a. Blackout
b. Air raid shelters – public and domestic

The Wardens network which ensured that people prepared their homes, and made their way to the shelters.

The blackout, imposed on September 1st 1939, and finally lifted, via period of partial blackout, on April 30th 1945, was perhaps the most intrusive aspect of air-raids defence, affecting anyone trying to move around after dark, and visible in white paint on lamp posts, curbs and on vehicles, including buses.

There were over 700 prosecutions for breach of blackout regulations in the first year of the war.[28]

Air Raid Sirens

Without adequate warning, no system of shelters or air raid precautions could work.

As will be seen in Chapter 3, the single raid on Reading which caused loss of life saw bombs falling almost simultaneously with the warning being sounded, catching people with no time to reach shelter. In a statement quoted by the *Reading Mercury* in September 1939, William McIlroy said that "five to seven minutes" warning would be available between the sirens going off and an attack happening. Anyone caught away from home (or, presumably their own shelter) could *If within a few minutes of his [sic] destination...probably try to reach it. Otherwise he should go to the nearest shelter as directed by wardens or the Police.*[29]

Air raid warnings were the responsibility of RAF Fighter Command, but the actual means of warning – sirens – were, again, the responsibility of the Corporation. By the end of October 1940 provision has been made for sixteen sirens across the Borough, in locations ranging from Tilehurst Water Tower to the "Co-op" jam factory in Coley. Sirens were operated by (at first) paid siren operator and the Police, who with Wardens also gave warnings in the streets. The locations of sirens established through Civil Defence Committee minutes are given in Appendix 6.

Siren tests occurred, at first, on the first Sunday in the month, but were discontinued during 1940. *The Berkshire Chronicle* reported the first use of the sirens at 7.32 on 6th September 1939, with an alert lasting just over 90 minutes brought about by the appearance of German aircraft off the East Coast.

Some gauge of the intrusiveness – or effectiveness – of the warning system comes from the County Siren and Warning log for 1940, which shows at least one alert over the central area of Berkshire every night from 9th September to 3rd October.[32]

Air Raid Shelters

Shelter building in Reading followed three phases

1. 1939-40 – Public shelters in the town centre

2. 1940-41 – Public shelters in residential areas and schools

3. 1941 – Public parks

Wardens' Post B8, St Michaels Church, Tilehurst, 2008.
Although the windows reflect conversion for use by the Police after the War, this is a standard purpose built Wardens' Post. The roof is concrete, the walls are reinforced brick. The standard pattern surface shelter was of a generally similar design.
(Author's photograph).

Early Closing Day

Britain's shelter building policy was shaped by the perceived nature of the threat, but also by the way the British lived.

In Germany, large communal shelters reflected the fact that in a city of any size most people lived in apartment blocks. It made sense to build large shelters, usually in the basements, to take them.

In general, greater ranges from enemy – especially British bases meant that a German town would receive more warning of attack, and so could gather people together.

In Reading, typically for the UK outside the centres of the major cities, people lived in individual houses. Although there would be a warning, this might be less than in Germany due to the shorter ranges involved (especially after the fall of France in June 1940). Hence, it made more sense for people to have individual shelters for each home. However, a massive campaign of shelter building was undertaken by the Corporation, beginning with trench shelters during the Munich Crisis of 1938, and resuming with basement shelters in September 1939.

At first these predominated in Reading, as the main form of attack was expected to be a short but intense raid launched in daylight. With people working in town, it made good sense to ensure that the main shopping streets were well provided for with shelters, and then to work out to the residential areas around. The Civil Defence Committee noted that *Priority was, naturally, given to the congested areas in the middle of the town.* [3]

In line with the perception that raids would come by day, and the recognition that most people would be in the Town Centre during "business hours" at first public shelters were open in the main in the daytime, although this would change with the experience of bombing.[34]

Alongside the official work, domestic shelters were built, and Anderson and Morrison shelters issued and sold.

Public shelters

Plans for the first public shelters were laid before the Civil Defence Committee before war had actually been declared. On 2nd September 1939 the Committee approved the Borough Surveyor's plans for shelters under Kings and Caversham Bridges and in the basements of properties in Broad Street. These basements – under numbers 4 (Blakey Morris), 38 (Hill and Farrer), 52-58 (A.H. Bull's) and 73 -74 (73 was Montague Burton's) – were requisitioned, with the Corporation able to claim government grant aid to offset the cost of *Reasonable expenditure up to £2380.*[35]

The requisitions themselves were noted by the Committee on the first day of the War, alongside land at the Laurels Tilehurst, Caversham Parochial School and under 40 Market place, all of which would be used for Civil Defence posts. The programme was extended to West Street, Station Approach and Holy Trinity Church in Oxford Rd by Mid September. By the 29th the Committee was able to record shelter places for over a thousand people approved.

Overground shelter building began in December 1939, with approval for shelters on Corporation land "where basements are not available". The option was felt to offer lower maintenance and compensation costs. The first three shelters were to be built on Christchurch Green, in Christchurch Gardens and in Church Street Caversham.

As shown in Appendix 5, by the time the main period of German bombing had ended, there were public shelters spaces for over 14,000 people, with another 1200 in shelters under construction.

In addition to shelters in the town itself, provision was made for public shelters in Reading's parks, suggested by the Chief Constable in August and approved on 30th October 1940, ranging from the accommodation for 50 people at Caversham Court, to over 1500 in shelters around Palmer Park.[36] In December 1939 the Committee heard that the standard trench shelter would be for fifty people, but shelters in parks were designed for up to 100. A number of these remain as bumps in the ground, with only that at Caversham Court still open. Schools received their own shelters, which would also serve the local community.

At first, all shelters were seen as *short term* places of refuge. Reading, in common with the rest of the UK, was caught out by the change in German bombing tactics which occurred in September 1940, with a switch from daylight to night time bombing. One result of this was demand for better, bomb proof shelters, but as shelters came to be used as places to retreat all night, this threw up the need for better provision and more comfort.

Although provision of bunks in public shelters was discussed, it was not until after the main threat had passed that the Corporation was able to react. On 10th December 1941, approval was given to convert the 100 seat shelter near Palmer Park Library *into a dormitory with concrete floors by Francis Bros (of Armour Road, Tilehurst) at a cost of £120*. Shelters at Tilehurst Triangle, Royal Berkshire Hospital and the Regal Cinema in Caversham were to follow.

A month later, the Civil Defence Committee approved £100 to provide a "Boiler tea urn, confectionary box, hot snack cupboard" for the Palmer Park dormitory

Early Closing Day

and the Vicar of St Bartholomew's was to be asked for volunteers to support the new provision.[37]

By autumn 1941 work on shelter construction was tailing off, and no new places were added between December 1941 and July 1942. By the end of 1942, the town had places for 99,058 people, which, depending on the measure used for population meant that, on the basis just of spaces available between c. 66 -100% of the people of Reading had access to a shelter space, with most provision in areas of highest threat and population density.

After this point some new provision was put in place, especially after the bombing of February 1943, but work concentrated on maintaining and improving existing public and domestic provision. On 4th May 1945, the Emergency Committee for Civil Defence noted receipt of the Ministry of Home Security's Circular 43/1945 ordering *The closure of all public and communal shelters upon the cessation of the risk of air attack and the demolition and relinquishment of shelters thereafter.*

Air raid shelter, Caversham Court, 2008.
This is the only public underground air raid shelter in Reading still in use, albeit as a store for Reading Borough Council. At the time the photograph was taken the shelter still had at least one of its original notices in place inside.
Built in 1941, it was designed to hold 50 people and was part of a set of shelters built in public parks.
(Author's photograph)

Chapter 1

Deep Shelters

One of the criticisms levelled at British preparations for bombing has been that the majority of shelters provided were not bomb proof. Most of the over ground shelters built by the Corporation were of reinforced brick with concrete slab roofs. Shelters in public parks were trenches lined and covered with concrete slabs.

Both types were heavily criticised during the War and afterwards, as experience in London, and elsewhere, showed that poor, or ill thought out, construction meant they were prone to collapse following a near miss by a bomb of any size. This was recognised in Reading at the time, and was the subject of a campaign by residents who described them as *Inadequate, highly dangerous, unsanitary [sic] and generally unwarranted.*[39]

In fairness, Reading was following contemporary best practice, misguided though it may have been, and the example of German cities where genuinely bomb proof shelters were built, suggests, that it would have been beyond Reading's means to provide such protection – German shelters, accommodating thousands of people featured wall and roofs of in many instances metres of reinforced concrete.[40]

Despite the scale of work done from the outbreak of war, the Corporation faced criticism of its efforts from across the Borough, with petitions for more shelter provision coming in from Tilehurst Ward Labour Association and Lower Caversham.[41] (Alongside this, in October 1940, the Chief Constable warned the Civil Defence Committee that "at present our great difficulty seems to be getting people to use the shelters")[42] In late 1940 and into summer 1941 consideration was given to what were described as "deep shelters" to be built in a chalk pit in Caversham.

The idea of deep shelters was prompted by a petition from more than 500 hundred residents of Battle Ward received by the Corporation in December 1940.[43] By that time bombs had fallen on the town and, with the Blitz at its height, residents were spending more and more nights in shelters.

The Battle Ward petition, referred to in a letter from the Town Clerk to the Ministry of Home Security dated 4th December 1940, requested

Strengthening of existing surface shelters, particularly at the base to make them blast proof as well as splinter proof and provision in them of lighting, heating and sanitary arrangements. b...a change over from the building of brick shelters to the first stage of the Haldane type of shelter...c...provision of bomb proof

Early Closing Day

shelters...[2nd Stage Haldane and] by tunnelling those areas of the town which are suitable

"Haldane" Shelters were named after the socialist Professor J.B.S Haldane, who, from WW1 onwards, and particularly inspired by the experience of bombing in the Spanish Civil War, called for large scale deep shelters that would be fully bomb proof.

The Corporation considered that "provision of shelters of the Haldane Type is not a practical proposition" and wanted the Ministry of Home Security to do this. However, an exchange of notes and calls between the Ministry and the Corporation showed that the idea had stuck. On the 19th of December the Ministry asked Reading to specify what use was being made of its existing shelters and what could be done at what cost to provide tunnel shelters. A note from July the following year shows that it was felt then that Reading had "plenty of leeway" to make up.

By early January the Borough Surveyor had visited the site under consideration, a chalk pit in Church Road Caversham, described as about 400 yards north of Caversham Bridge. Despite the public request for Haldane shelters, his report to the Ministry's Regional Technical adviser warned that there was up to this moment ... *no clear evidence in Reading of a desire to sleep underground.*[44]

However, the site was suitable and it was felt offered the possibility of tunnels to accommodate up to 15,000 people, beneath 68ft of chalk. Such a shelter, costing around £8-10 per head could offer sanitation, recreation and first aid provision.

How seriously the Corporation took this idea is not clear, and discussions carried on into the summer, when the Ministry noted, perhaps a little grumpily that "the Corporation obviously want us to make up their minds for them". Cost, a shortage of labour and a lack of perceived need killed the scheme off in September 1941.

Andersons and Morrisons

Whilst the brick and concrete surface shelters drew criticism, and "Haldane" shelters were beyond practical reach, the far simpler Anderson and Morrison shelters provided for domestic use, have been praised and are widely (if not always fondly) remembered.

By 1942, Reading had provided almost 7000 Anderson shelters and 750 Morrisons.

The Anderson was named after Sir John Anderson pre-war Lord Privy Seal, with responsibility for Civil Defence (later Viscount Waverley, and on the outbreak of war the Home Secretary and Minister of Home Security). [45]

Supplied in kit form, it was a simple set of curved corrugated iron panels, with a front and back plate to be bolted together and dug into the ground. With a covering of fifteen inches of earth, it was expected to be splinter and rubble proof, but in practice the shelters proved surprisingly resistant to even near misses.

The Pocket Guide to the Air Raid Precautions arrangements in Reading, issued in early 1940, noted *Anderson shelters, if they are properly earthed over, give protection against many dangerous occurrences, except of course, a direct hit.* [46]

In March 1940, Reading's Civil Defence Committee noted that they came in "Standard, small and extension A and B", offering six seat with four in the small and eight or ten in the extended version. A number still survive in back gardens doing duty as sheds after over seventy five years.

On the 1st September 1939, the Home Office wrote to the Civil Defence Emergency Committee saying that it could deliver ten "garden shelters "as exhibition specimens".[47] Issue of free four-seater Andersons was authorised on 24th October. Other sizes had to be paid for - £5 or £7 depending on the income of the head of the household (assumed to be a man). Households could opt not to have one The Corporation's Pocket Book on ARP issued in early 1940 implies that council houses were being built with shelters – presumably Andersons provision, but at the time of writing this has not been verified.

Final approval for the issue of Anderson shelters was given by the Committee in February 1940, with the Ministry of Home Security stating that it would supply four hundred small sized and two hundred standard sized units, increasing within days to six hundred small and one hundred and fifty standard. As the shelters needed to be dug in by about four feet, the Borough Surveyor was instructed to state where "water in the soil" would make Andersons impossible to use.[48]

With demand assessed at 13,585 units, and by the end of February 1940, 1900 shelters on the way, the Committee had to set priorities. Its decision illustrates the areas seen as most at threat. First priority went to the Orts Road area and New Town, then that part of Battle Ward "west of the Great Western Railway" (effectively the homes along and north of the Oxford Road) and then to Katesgrove.[49]

As with other shelters the paradigm that the Anderson was designed to meet – short daylight raids – proved invalid, and by autumn 1940 the small size, four seater shelters were proving inadequate as people had begun to sleep in them.

Early Closing Day

The Corporation began to issue extension sets, and by mid 1941 was the Highways Department was fabricating its own using material supplied by the Ministry of Home Security.

By 1942 enough spaces in Anderson shelters were available to accommodate more than 26,000 people, about one in four of the population.

Although effective, Andersons were not always popular – in 1943 the Civil Defence Committee heard that a Mrs Haines, of Katesgrove, wanted her Anderson removed. Wardens sent to assist covering it in earth found it "still full of house refuse".[50]

Often derided, and frequently misunderstood, the Morrison shelter arrived in Reading from mid 1941.

Designed to give every home an indoor shelter, avoiding the problems of communal shelters and garden shelters, the "Morrison" was a deceptively simple box of steel sections, bolted together and covered in heavy mesh. Large enough to sleep a family, the little structures proved astonishingly resistant to the collapse of their parent building, and even to blast. Named after Herbert Morrison, who took over from Sir John Anderson as Home Secretary, it was officially the "Table (Morrison) Indoor Shelter" (it could be used as a rather large bulky dining room table).

Arriving at the end of the main period of threat, relatively little appears in the Emergency Committee minutes about the Morrison, and whilst they provided around 2000 shelter places by May 1942, it is hard to gain an impression of their impact.

By the Civil Defence Committee meeting of 21 July 1941, 750 Morrison shelters had been received, with 250 delivered free of charge. A further twenty six had been paid for. Large families could buy an extra shelter, and in March 1942, delivery began of two tier shelters.[51] However, as late as July 1944, the Borough Surveyor was to report that although the Borough had a stock of thirty three single tier and five double tier Morrisons, the Regional Technical advisers had said that *No more will be forthcoming for Reading as they are in very short supply and all of the available shelters are being collected and distributed in the more vulnerable areas.*[52]

The threat had now changed to the V1 flying bomb – and as Chapter Two will show, Reading was effectively – if not completely - out of range.

Air Raid Precautions

Perhaps the most easily recognised of the Civil Defence services today, the Wardens Service, was a key aspect of not only reaction to an air raid, but of developing protection against one.[53]

Given their visibility and close involvement in Reading's experience of the threat of bombing, and, of course, their involvement in dealing with the effects of air raids, it's worth looking at the Wardens Service in some detail.

The 1940 Pocket Guide to ARP in Reading summarised their role as reporting damage and *Shepherding the public and preventing panic.*[54]

The number of wardens was laid down by central government. ARP circular 14/1939 stated that full time wardens should make up to 20% of the total personnel with two paid wardens, one per shift, covering three sectors.[55] Later this was amended by Home Service Circular 58/1940 to two paid wardens per post and ten per square mile.[56]

In July 1940 Reading reported to HQ No6 Area that it had

- 984 male wardens (over 40)
- 246 female wardens[57]

Most wardens were part time volunteers, initially to be paid 10/- per week and for time lost. Head Wardens were paid more - £3-15s in 1941. Senior wardens were paid £3-12s with the female counter parts £2-9s.[58] In one week in September 1939, the total wage bill in Reading for Wardens alone came to £709.[59] Correspondence in the National Archives shows a period of regular jockeying over costs between local and central government.

The basis of recruitment for ARP Wardens changed over time in response to the threat. In theory, from the start of the war, conscription for part-time ARP work was possible, although at first the lack of threat meant that this was not needed. From June 1940, men from 30 to 50 who were eligible for conscription could opt to serve in Civil Defence and in October 1940 – with the Blitz approaching its height – paid Warden's jobs were "frozen" so that a warden could not resign without permission. By 1942 registration for service in the auxiliary forces (such as the Army's Auxiliary Territorial Service (ATS), Land Army, specified war industries or Civil Defence became compulsory for unmarried women aged between twenty and thirty one.

Early Closing Day

The numbers involved are striking. In October 1941 the total number of wardens available was in Reading 1375.[60] As discussed below, ARP Wardens were organised into "Groups" and individual Posts. Reporting on the 1943 raid, Group A (covering Caversham) reported 52 wardens and two messengers on duty, Group D (right under the bombs in that raid, in the town centre), 39. In the log book of Post A7, on the Woodcote Road in Caversham, the last day of peace (Sept. 2nd 1939) saw six wardens on duty in a given shift, with a note of an instruction that the post was to be "manned all day and night with either two wardens or one warden and one messenger. Four Wardens to be in readiness for patrol duty"[61]

Anderson Shelter, Caversham, March 1940. According to the original caption this is Mr. A. G. Reynolds, of River Road, with his – literally – shiny new Anderson. This would one one of the earliest examples delivered. There is still a lot of work to do, as if it's not possible to dig the shelter in by three feet or so, at least the covering of at least 15 inches of earth needs completing. (Reading Libraries 1267064)

Wardens' Posts

For ARP purposes, Reading was divided into nine areas – A to I, each split into up to twenty five sectors. In charge of each area was a Head Warden, responsible for up to nine posts.

Details of this system from 1940 are given in Appendix 3, but the approximate coverage of the Groups was

Group A – Caversham

Group B – Tilehurst

Group C – West Reading

Group D – the town centre and north to Caversham

Group E – the southern part of the town centre and Coley

Group F – Katesgrove

Group G – Whitley

Group H – between the town centre and the area around Royal Berkshire
       Hospital

Group I – Newtown and the area around Palmer Park

The Wardens' Post was the key local manifestation of Air Raids Precautions, and a full list is also given in Appendix 3. Reading's guide to ARP stated

Each post has a telephone and is protected against splinter and blast [and] all reports of air raid damage will be made to the reporting centre

Wardens' post must be regarded by the general public as the local HQ of the ARP... [gives] children's respirators and babies protective helmets.[62]

The post itself could vary from a room in a pub, or even a private home, to an underground dug-out or specially built brick and concrete structure. Land was appropriated for specially built posts – for example on 14th September 1939, the Emergency and Civil Defence Committee noted the requisition of land in a meadow off Allcroft Road, near the Mount, for a post, which would become "F4", needing an area 20ft by 35ft. [63]

The land on which Post A7 was built on, at the junction of Woodcote Way and Woodcote Road, was appropriated on 29th September and n December 1939 the Committee paid Messers T.A. Fisher and Sons £5 to remove part of a large apple tree that was interfering with Post I1 at 59a Cholmeley Road, Newtown.[64]

Conditions in the posts varied. In March 1940 it was noted that H Group had been using the Eldon Arms as a post. On the other hand, in October that year, the Civil Defence Committee heard that at Post B6 (Tilehurst Triangle) it *was impossible for the head warden to carry on his work...[and impossible to enlarge the post] owing to the ground being waterlogged.* [65]

B6 continued to cause problems – almost three years later the Civil Defence committee considered a request to move it to the garage of the Prince of Wales pub, a few yards away, as the wooden floor had collapsed due to dry rot. The Committee approved £10 to concrete the floor. [66]

Similar problems were reported from Posts B4 in Armour Hill, Tilehurst and G2 in Northumberland Avenue on the other side of town. [67]

In fairness, the entire ARP network had been created from virtually nothing, and gone from planning to a network of over forty posts in barely three months, and work began early to ensure that wardens had, at least, basic comfort.

Early Closing Day

Two days before War was declared, the Emergency Committee instructed the Borough Accountant to buy a "primus stove, kettle, teapot and drinking utensils" for each post and the ARP Officers was to "make representations" to get cost of this paid for by Government and to report on food for posts. This was to be food to be cooked by electric cookers at Corporation Highway depot at Caversham Road and other depots in Caversham and Tilehurst. [68]

On 14th September, the log of Post A7 noted that they had been provided with "tea, sugar, milk, sandwiches, sausage rolls" twice daily, enough "to keep two persons going for 12 hrs"

Less than a month later, the Committee approved £68/8/9 for seventy five folding beds, and £20 for "sanitation heat and light". [70]

In Coley, after wardens of Post E6 — by the Shaw Road entrance to the Recreation Ground (now Coley Park)- had asked to have a water supply in their post, the Allotment Holders Water Committee offered to make their tap (which was right next to the Post) available to them if the *ARP authorities would make some sort of gesture in the way of a small donation...* [71]

Wardens were trained – the Emergency Committee minutes refer to staff going on training courses regularly – with local instruction happening in a hall in Silver Street. In October 1939, the Curator of Museum and Art Gallery was authorised to spend £66 from Education Committee funds for films for the ARP.

At first, in addition to basic equipment – a helmet, respirators and tools – wardens had only armbands as uniform. These were bought from Langston's and Sons for 3s 1 ½ for ten.[72] Finally, uniforms were supplied in August 1941. An authorisation for the purchase of uniforms survives in the Committee minutes for 16th October 1942 – including 130 women's jacket's at 30/6d each, and the same number of great coats at 42s each.

Something of the day-to-day work of a Warden's post can be gathered from the log book of Post A7 at Westdene on the Upper Woodcote Road in Caversham, already quoted above. The log survives for the period August 31st 1939 to 11th September 1940. [73] Excerpts only are given here.

Aug 31st 1939 – Manned at 6.30, and equipment arrived 8.10

Sept 1st - 7 staff on duty 18-30-0500 next morning.

Sept 6th – Yellow warning at 7.10

- Report of Bright lights at No1 Blixton Avenue

Sept 8th – Pay envelopes

Nov 16th – Key for lavatory in new post

Nov 21st – RAF exercise over Reading 10am-2.30 "best to let people know this so that they will not be nervous"

With the launch of the German offensive against France and the Low Countries in May 1940, what feels like comfortable domestic routine changed for the team at Upper Woodcote Road.

May 12th – 14.10 Members of the Civil Defence Service who see parachutists should immediately report same to the police

May 26th – "LDV (Local Defence Volunteers) personnel be allowed to use any ARP telephones in emergency"

July 2nd – Message from Group HQ "making preparations to defend town". With reference to Reading, from 5pm tonight male ...volunteers to assist in filling sandbags at gravel pit behind post B2 (rec'd 19.25) The log closes with a note of sirens over the town on 6th September 1940.

During raids on Reading two wardens posts were hit – Post E4 was damaged in 1940, and Post D5 was knocked out by the bomb that destroyed the People's Pantry in 1943.

Gas Detection and Identification Services

One area of Air Raid Precautions that is genuinely hard for a modern researcher to appreciate is the seriousness with which gas attack was taken. The United Kingdom was prepared to use chemical weapons in a future war, and fully expected them to be used against its civilian population in World War Two

In addition to gas masks for every citizen (from 1938) and detailed information on how to prepare a home for gas attack, Reading's ARP services made specific provision for gas attack. At first the distribution of gas masks was free, coordinated from the Instruction Centre in Silver Street, mentioned above as the main ARP training centre, but soon replacement masks were charged for – ranging from 2/6 for the loss of an adult respirator, to 25 shillings for a full baby helmet. [74]

The Gas Detection and Identification Service was established within the ARP framework on 4th September 1939.[75] Gas Identification officers included specialist chemists, controlled via the Report and Control Centre, whose role was to advise Wardens on identifying any gas bombs. [76] At the start of the war the three advisers were Dr. D.R. Maxted, Dr. Paul White and Mr. K.S. Fowler, all from the University of Reading. By the end of September all three had transferred to the Regional centre.[77]

Specially erected posts, and even the tops of pillar boxes, were covered in yellow-green gas detecting paint which changed colour when exposed to spray gasses. The log of Wardens' Post A7 records that on 26th September 1939, locations were selected in its sector at

> Sector A7a
>
> Methodist Church at corner of Highmoor and Woodcote Rd.
>
> Pillar box corner of St Peters Ave and Woodnote Rd
>
> Pillar box corner Harrogate Rd and Woodcote Rd
>
> A7b
>
> 149 Woodcote Rd
>
> Pillar box Upper Woodcote Rd and Shepherds Lane

The post itself held a range of anti-gas equipment, ranging from full protective suits to tins of anti-dimming cream for the lenses in gas masks. Oddly, its inventory lists only "right hand gloves". In 1947, when it was disposing of civil defence stores, the Committee sold off a range of materials including 735 one-hundredweight drums of bleaching powder – held for use against mustard gas.[78]

Wardens themselves were given anti-gas training – fixed gas chambers for this purpose were approved in November 1939, with portable "Smoke Huts" for training installed in Percy Place, Greyfriars School, at the "rear of S Reading Library and Norcot Rd School" [79] In addition to these, a bus was taken out of service and converted for use as a mobile "gas chamber" to allow training for the public.[80]

At Post A7, in the second month of the war, instructions were received that one of two of its women wardens was to attend Post 2 to be instructed in the fitting of babies respirators so that *they will be able to explain this to the mothers*. Post A2 was in the then Caversham Parochial School in School Lane. In November the post took charge of fifty full protective helmets for babies, and in February 1940, forty of the colourful "Mickey Mouse" children's respirators arrived.[81]

In addition to detection and protection, the Corporation provided for the decontamination of streets, homes, animals and clothing. As noted below, decontamination teams were included alongside rescue parties and West Reading Laundry, and other premises were to be used for decontamination.

Caversham brick works was to be used to store unexploded gas bombs.[82]

Anti-gas exercises were held regularly, and gas attacks featured in civil defence drills. In December 1939, for example, a simulated raid on Tilehurst covering personnel from eleven ARP Posts assumed that three enemy aircraft had dropped five 500lb high explosive bombs, three 1kg incendiaries and also three 50lb gas bombs.[83] Tear gas was used in the town centre in August 1941 as part of a joint military and civil defence exercise.[84]

Reading Borough Police [85]

Based in Valpy Street, Reading's police force was integral to the ARP services. The Chief Constable – for much of the war, Thomas Burrows – reported regularly both to the Civil Defence Committee and the Watch Committee on civil defence issues. (He was also responsible for the Fire Service in Reading).

With 159 officers, it found itself stretched by an influx of new residents as evacuees, both adults and children, arrived and later with the arrival of increasing numbers of servicemen. Men were lost to the Forces and yet the Police still took on a wide range of additional duties – for example "sharp blasts" on police whistles were use as a warning of gas attack. [86]

As the incidents described in Chapters 2 and 3 will show, police officers were often first on the scene of any attack, and senior members of the force acted as Incident Officers, coordinating and controlling the response at the scene. This is shown well in the bombing raid on Caversham on 26th November 1940, with constables reporting incidents, and an Inspector establishing an Incident post. More widely, in 1943, the Chief Constable told the Corporation's Watch Committee that 285 Special Constables had been trained in anti-gas measures.[87]

In addition to Special Constables, the Force called on the First Police Reserve and Police War Reserve to add to numbers. The former was made up of retired policemen, the second of volunteers who undertook regular training, but would be called up as paid officers in wartime.

Three Reading police officers were killed whilst in the Forces, and PC. Rex Jupp was killed in 1943 during the People's Pantry bombing raid.

The Home Guard

Locally available records for Reading's Home Guard are patchy, and the Home Guard came under Army and thence War Office control, not that of Civil Defence. However, given the simple fact of their existence as an organised body, with men on duty and on call, the Home Guard was closely involved in

Early Closing Day

responding to incidents – for example in raids on Caversham in 1940 and on the town centre in 1943.

At first the Home Guard were all volunteers, but from 1942 compulsory registration – effectively conscription - was introduced for men from 18 to 51 in areas where the Home Guard was under strength.

Reading raised two Battalions of the Home Guard:

7th Berkshire (Reading Borough) under Lt. Col. G.S. Field

10th (Reading Post Office) under Lt.Col. H.C. Gray

There were neighbouring battalions covering, for example, Wokingham and Pangbourne, and the 12th Battalion was formed by the Upper Thames Patrol operating boats on the River itself. Companies or platoons within a battalion could be raised by individual work places or localities. Berkshire Record Office holds, for example photographs of the Woodley Platoon, Reading Transport and from the Huntley and Palmers Home Guard.

These battalions, which varied in size according to the area they covered (unlike a Territorial or Regular Army Battalion) formed part of the Berkshire Zone, later known as the Berkshire Group,[88] and were administered by the local Territorial Army Association, operating from Yeomanry House on Tilehurst Road.

At some point from May 1942 some of Berkshire's Home Guard were formed into 198 (101 Berkshire Home Guard) Anti Aircraft "Z" Battery as part of the Berkshire and Buckinghamshire Anti-Aircraft Group under Royal Artillery control, manning the rocket projectors mentioned above. The Battery commander was Maj. T.W. Vanderpump, and the shortage of officers listed in the *Home Guard List* for September 1942 suggests that the Battery had only just been formed at that point.[89] From this source it is impossible to tell to what extent the Battery included Reading men.

The Minutes from the Civil Defence Committee also contain a suggestion that the Home Guard was actively supporting ARP at the very least at the level of the equivalent of fire watching. At its meeting on 12th December 1940 the Committee heard that the Home Guard had set up what were described as "lookout posts manned nightly". Their purpose isn't given, but the fact that they were drawn to the Committee's attention, with a note that their reports were "poor" seems to show that their role was in dealing with air raids. No further mention is made of these.

In 1943 the Home Guard was discussed as an additional source of manpower for the new Fire Guard service. [90]

Conversely, civil defence personnel were given weapons training and would have been expected to play a role in defending the Town. [91]

Dealing with the effects of bombing

Once a raid had occurred, civil defence services were organised to

1. Deal with any casualties

2. Fight fires

3. Rescue people and deal with initial damage

4. Provide food, information and practical support to anyone de-housed.

Casualty Services

First Aid Posts

A First Aid Post was equipped and staffed for the treatment of "walking wounded" and those affected by persistent poison gasses. They were constantly staffed. In September 1939, total staffing provided was 40 men and 200 women, with posts at

1. Caversham Parochial School, School Lane

2. The Laurels, School Rd, Tilehurst

3. Grovelands School, Oxford Rd

4. ARP Instructional Centre, Silver St

5. Whitley Clinic, Northumberland Ave.

6. Newtown Infants School, School Terrace

7. Battle Hospital.

The role was vital, as many casualties were expected, and the Royal Berkshire and Battle Hospitals could easily have been overwhelmed. In any case, this structure followed the pattern of putting ARP services where people were, instead of centralising them.

Originally, casualties were to be allocated between the two hospitals in the ratio of 2: 1 between the "Royal Berks" and Battle, but following the casualties and

Early Closing Day

experience of the raid on the Town Centre on 10th February 1943, it was decided that in future for every casualty sent to Battle Hospital four would go to the Royal Berkshire Hospital. [92]

First Aid Party and Ambulance Depots

The First Aid Posts provided points to which anyone injured but mobile could go or be taken. Relief on the scene of an "incident" was offered by First Aid Parties and ambulances. A First Aid Party was a team of five, with transport. In 1939 a Region 6 return noted thirty five in Reading, with 165 staff, half of these full time paid staff. [93]

Reading supported 50 ambulances, and 33 cars for sitting casualties, staffed by 266 female drivers; 15% of the staff were full time paid. [94] First aid and ambulance services were the responsibility of Mr C.A.Poole, the County Commissioner of the St John's Ambulance and the Medical Officer for Health.[95]

First Aid Party Depots [96]

Castle Depot – 113 Castle Hill

Foxley Depot – 25 Redlands Rd.

Caversham Deport – Caversham Parochial School

Ambulance Depots

Caversham Motors, Church St. Caversham

Hewens Garage, Castle St

Jarvis Garage, Christchurch Rd.

Provision was made for an expected heavy level of casualties, with mortuaries taken over, or even rented, from commercial concerns.

Fire [97]

Before 1938 there was no statutory requirement for a local authority to operate or provide a fire service.

Reading's own fire service was established as a separate entity in 1893 and became the core of a much expanded service during wartime. The "regulars", based at the then new fire station on Caversham Road (it opened in 1939, replacing the original in St Mary's Butts), provided training for the new Auxiliary Fire Service as well as day to day cover.

Chapter 1

In 1940, the Controller of the Fire Service was the Chief Constable, T.A Burrows, the Chief Officer E.F, Batchford.[98]

Speaking in 1938, Chief Officer Batchford summed up the Fire Brigades expectation of what was to come *in the case of incendiary bombs being used that would mean 100-200 fires at once...Last year the Brigade dealt with 108.* [99]

Supporting them, the volunteer Auxiliary Fire Service (AFS) provided cover across the town. The AFS was set up under the same Air Raids Precautions Act of 1937 as the other civil defence services and membership was voluntary, although firemen were paid £3 a week in wartime. Membership was based around men aged 25-30, serving full or part time. Women over 18 were used as drivers and in control room duties – although they received basic fire fighting training, from 1942 at least, based in Maidenhead. [100]

The Auxiliary Fire Service in Reading was divided into six areas with sub stations at

No 1 area –   Central Section – Old Fire Station, St Mary's Butts

No 2 and 4 areas – South Section – Gowrings Garage London Rd

No 3 area –   Eastern Section – Thames Valley Garage, London Rd

No 5 area –   Tilehurst Section Prince of Wales Pub, Park Lane; Shepherd and Carters' Garage

No 6 area –   Caversham Section – Caversham Court

Other part-time stations were added during the war – for example at Bakers Garage off Friar Street, with "action stations" around Reading, for example in the area of Balmore Drive, Caversham.[101]

Next to wardens, auxiliary firemen made up the second highest element in the ARP wage bill in the first month of the war, and as Alan Sandall makes clear, they came to take on more and more work. *Are you 17?*, Alan Sandall's lightly fictionalised autobiography is perhaps the most detailed and vivid account of the world of one of the civil defence services for Reading at this time. This is fortunate, as at the time of writing, little has come out of the official Civil Defence and other Corporation records to shed light on this important area and much published material is anecdotal.

In 1941 all fire brigades in Britain, together with the Auxiliary Fire Service were joined as the National Fire Service (NFS), with Berkshire Buckinghamshire and Oxfordshire coming under the NFS's "15 Fire Force", one of what eventually became forty two such Forces across the country. Reading was "A Division", with a base at the Mansion House in Prospect Park. A division was intended to

Early Closing Day

comprise 100 fire pumps (and their towing vehicles).

Interviewed in 2002, Norman Kent, who was a messenger with the National Fire Service, listed the stations in Reading of A Division as

15 A 1 O – Friar Street – a part time location near Merchants Place

15 A 1 U – Oxford Road/Junction Road

15 A 1 V – Caversham Court

15 A 1 W – Wokingham Road/Hamilton Road

15 A 1 X – London Road/Pell Street

15 A 1 Y – St Mary's Butts

15 A 1 Z – Caversham Road [102]

Fire fighting depended on a supply of water. Large tanks were set up at various points around Reading, and sources of natural water identified. Alan Sandall, who was in the National Fire Service, writes of "a massive dam" near Tilehurst Station connected by a pipeline and pump to the Thames together with fifty one other locations where pumps could be installed to relay water.[103] Other points across Reading were identified as water sources, and the painted, if fading, signs locating some of these can occasionally be seen.

Surprisingly, one "dam" caused problems with a local air raid shelter. In April 1943 the Emergency and Invasion Committee heard that the National Fire Service had installed a 5000 gallon tank at St George's Church (in St George's Road, off the Oxford Road in West Reading). Unfortunately, an error in siting had led to the tank being placed "over part of the underground shelter for school children". The NFS were instructed to move the "dam" to its intended position against the west wall of the Church.[104]

In the event, with few air-raids and only perhaps one or two involving incendiaries, Reading's firemen and women saw more action outside the town. Crews were sent to major raids from London and Southampton to Coventry, Birmingham and Bristol. For one raid on London in 1940-41, the Caversham Road Fire Station also acted as collecting point and temporary base for eighty-eight appliances from other brigades en-route to the Capital.[105] However, as incident reports in Chapter 2 show, when needed Reading could itself call on fire crews from neighbouring areas.

Fire Watchers, Supplementary Fire Parties and Fire Guard

Supporting the warden's and fire service was perhaps the most numerous of

Reading's ARP services, the Fire Guard.

From September 1940, in common with the rest of the country, all men under 63 not otherwise involved in civil defence or Home Guard duties – and later all women under 45 - had to perform fire watching duty, and all major concerns had to have staff available for duty out of hours. This involved duty at the individual's place of work, reporting fires to the ARP services, and dealing with individual incendiaries.

Although never compulsory, residents were encouraged to form Supplementary Fire Parties to fight fires in their own streets. Again, in addition to their normal working hours, Dave Doe notes that in a major exercise in 1941 fire watchers or Fire Guards were sucked into dealing with incendiary bombs at the end of a night's shift.[106]

From 1941, following wider experience of fire bombing, the Fire Guard, at first part of the ARP Services, was established subsuming the existing Supplementary Fire Parties. Enrolment was compulsory, and extended to women in 1942.

Under the Head Fire Guard – Mr. F.B. Gleave, Headmaster of Battle School – street fire parties of twenty to thirty people operated in teams of three on duty during, and just on either side of, blackout hours. Training was given – in Reading this was supervised by Arthur Negus – and the aim was to provide a "stirrup pump", for use on individual incendiary bombs for every thirty or so homes.

In 1943 the Fire Guard was moved from ARP to become a free standing organisation under the National Fire Service. The new organisation *Would not relieve wardens of their general responsibility for reporting the fall of bombs...to the report centre.* [107]

Civil Defence Committee minutes for the period show that reorganising and establishing the new service took up considerable time and effort.

The new-look Fire Guard was based around six offices in addition to its main office at 11 Duke Street. These were at:

Caversham Senior School

Whitley Park School

Alfred Sutton School

Battle School

Norcot School [108]

Early Closing Day

It was organised into eleven areas – shadowing the Warden's Groups – and in addition to the Fire Guard Officer and a Deputy had eight Assistant Fire Guard Officers. There were to be 155 sectors with Area Officers covering fifteen each, Area Captains, five.[109] Provision was made for 700 steel helmets for Fire Guards with uniform for Officers, who were to be paid.

From September 1944, with German bombers further and further out of range with Allied advances across Europe, the Fire Guard was scaled down. [110]

Fire Watchers on duty in Wellsteeds department store were amongst those injured in the bombing of February 1943.

Rescue and Repair

Working under the Borough Surveyor, Reading had three Heavy Rescue parties and three Light Rescue Parties. Each was 9-11 men under a superintendent with a "skilled foreman". These dealt with the "rescue of injured persons who may be trapped in damaged buildings".

In addition there were three decontamination squads of seven men each with a superintendent and leader and three road and sewer repair parties, also seven men under a leader

As with other ARP services, the rescue and repair arm was based in locations across the Borough, allowing a quick response to incidents at the expense of time spent concentrating parties for larger incidents.

Central Depot – Abattoirs Rd

Light rescue

Heavy rescue

Decontamination

Road and sewer repair

Caversham Depot – Gosbrook Road

Light rescue

Heavy rescue

Decontamination

Tilehurst Depot – Norcot Rd

Light rescue

Heavy rescue

Decontamination

Road and sewer repair

Chapter 1

Emmer Green Depot

Road and sewer repair.

From October 1943, ambulance and rescue parties were amalgamated. [111]

Information and Advice

Provision of information was organised by Emergency Information Officers from the Corporation and the Ministries of Information and Health. According to the 1942 edition of *Measures necessary after heavy air attack* they were "publicity agents for Government Departments and Local Authority" and were also to "take such steps as necessary to uphold morale". [112] Information was provided through five centres, staffed from the Corporation and the voluntary sector.

- Palmer Hall West Street.

- Trinity Congregational Institute, Sidmouth Street.

- Oxford Hall, Eaton Place

- Caversham Senior School

- Whitley Community Centre, Northumberland Avenue

- Congregational Church Hall, Armour Road, Tilehurst

In addition to these government providers of information, the local Citizens' Advice Bureau – at Watlington House, 44 Watlington Street – was included in the overall network, giving advice including "Evacuation, rent, HP, Mortgages..."

The Corporation also provided information in its own right, including the booklet *Pocket Guide to ARP...* which is an important source for this chapter.

Opening of People's Pantry, December 1940. The Mayor collects a plate of food from the servery in 175 Friar Street, the newly opened People's Pantry. The woman to his right, in Women's Voluntary Service uniform is probably Dorothy Deans, the Reading Centre Organisers. Her volunteers staffed the People's Pantry. (Reading Museum REDMG : 1980.36.A448.5. Copyright Reading Museum (Reading Borough Council). All rights reserved).

Early Closing Day

Posters were issued and, for example, on the third day of the war 30,000 leaflets were to be sent out calling for ARP volunteers.[113]

Food

Region 6 made extensive provision for feeding displaced people and victims in the event of a major attack.[114]   Under the Wartime Meals Division of the Ministry of Food, food in the area was to be provided by

- "British Restaurants" at
a. The People's Pantry in Friar St.,

b. Kings Road,

c. Oxford Hall,

d. Gosbrook Road

e. Northumberland Avenue

- Emergency Feeding Centres

- Mobile canteens

- Cooking depots

The King's Road British Restaurant is remembered as

Ambulance from Reading, Pennsylvania, 1940. Seen in his full regalia, accompanied by the Deputy Mayor, Alderman Alice Jenkins and the Mace Bearer, William McIllroy takes ownership of an ambulance donated by women from Reading Pennsylvania. The vehicle was eventually passed to the Royal Berkshire Hospital.
(Reading Libraries 1289044)

being next to the Liberal Club. Interviewed in 2002, Frances Greary described it as "spartan to say the least". [115]

A British Restaurant was a "standard feeding centre operated by the local authority... [which also act as] Emergency Feeding Centres".

The aim was to give 10% of the population twelve meals over three or four days.[116]

With industrial works canteens and school meals widespread, an important aim of British Restaurants (the name was chosen by Churchill, who didn't like the more prosaic "Emergency Feeding Centre") was to allow workers who did not have access to a works canteen – for example the shop workers of Reading town centre – access to a cheap meal to help make their rations go further. In 1918, three "Communal Kitchens" had performed a similar role in Reading, but on what we would call a "take away" basis.[117]

However, it is clear that not all Emergency Feeding Centres were to act in the fashion of the British Restaurants. A further Emergency Feeding Centre was under discussion in May 1941, to be located at the Snowflake Laundry in Caversham. Whitley Special School (subsequently the Avenue School), Pendragon Hall School were also discussed, and centres were to be set up at the Oratory School – later to be discussed as moving to St Barnabas Church Hall and Suttons Seeds Trial Grounds.[118] At one point in 1942 it was suggested that Woolworth's in Broad Street would be used.[119]

It's also not clear of all the British Restaurants mentioned were in operation simultaneously – mention of the one in Gosbrook Road doesn't appear until September 1943 (although it may have been in operation before) and the Womens' Voluntary Service report on the destruction of the People's Pantry speaks of only two other British Restaurants – Kings Road and Oxford Road.[120]

Records from the Housing Committee refer to a "British Restaurants Sub Committee" which was in existence at least in 1941 and still meeting in 1944.[121] The Sub Committee is not referred to in the Civil Defence Committee minutes and at the time of writing it is not clear of which Committee this was a sub-committee.

The best known – apparently both in popular memory and at the time – of the British Restaurants, The People's Pantry, was opened on 11th December 1940 by Lady Northampton.[122] It functioned on a day-to-day basis as an ordinary restaurant, with its own kitchens in the basement. However, as an Emergency Feeding Centre, it was equipped to feed anyone who lost their own access to cooking due to a serious air raid. As such it would have held

Teas, sugar, condensed milk, baked beans, soup, canned meat and margarine sufficient to feed 10% of the population with 12 meals per head" over a three-four day period. Canned food was to be supplemented by milk and bread from local firms. [123]

During the immediate aftermath of the worst bombing in Reading, that of February 1943, two British Restaurants supplied rescue workers from the regional pools, and mortuary and rest centre staff with 7000 sandwiches and 40 gallons of soup and other drinks.[124]

Fresh food would be supplied by the nearest Cooking Depot in insulated containers. Reading's nearest were in Wantage and Bracknell, (Victoria Cross Hall and Church House respectively). A Cooking depot could supply a steady flow of 3000 meals every two hours, with an emergency rate of 6000 possible in a four hour period. Capacity for Berkshire was stated as being 17000 people

Early Closing Day

per meal. Emergency Feeding Centres could be replenished with full stocks within 12 hours, with the effort coordinated by the Divisional Office of the Ministry of Food based at 61 Bath Road.

In May 1943, 226 Northumberland Avenue was brought into use as a store for the British Restaurants.[125] The Corporation's Civil Defence committee discussed setting up mobile canteens and their minutes give a note on the stocks of food to be provided. On 25th May 1941 a new mobile canteen was presented by a Mr John Messias. It was stocked with

28lbs sugar - 20lbs tea - 108 tins stew etc   -   156 tins soup - 60 tins milk

144 tins cocoa - 12 tins herrings - Bread from Co-op Bakery

Cost £18/3/6 [126]

Supporting this were national "columns" under the control of the Queen's Messenger, with ten specially fitted vehicles to provide an emergency "surge" of 16,000 meals over three to four days.

Rest Centres

Provision as made for somewhere for the homeless – temporary or longer term – to rest and get basic food bedding and clothing. Emergency Rest Centres were set up by "Public Assistance authorities".[127] With 1400 such centres, No6 Region had provision for 120,000 people by 1942. 16,500 places were available in Berkshire, with 3000 around Reading and 5000 places in the area covered by the Borough Corporation. Shinfield School, for example, offered 100 places. Centres in the immediate area noted by the Southern Regional Commissioner were at

Arborfield	Benham
Winnersh	Bradfield
Wargrave	Woolhampton
Twyford	Streatley
Pangbourne	Theale
Wokingham	Burghfield
Mortimer	

In Reading itself, there was a Rest Centre at Palmer Hall Sick Benefit Club at 42 West St.

Berkshire County Council noted the stocks held by these centres in 1945 -

2956 small chairs - 38,400 blankets - 16,000 dinner plates

11,856 tins of baked beans - 1235 tins of pilchards. [128]

The WVS

It is hard to overestimate the contribution of the Women's Voluntary Service – now the Royal Voluntary Service - to preparations for and action after bombing in Reading. These can only be sketched in here.[129]

Formed as the Women's Voluntary Service for Civil Defence, it was established by Lady Reading in May 1938. Locally 1200 members joined between November 1938 and 1940.

Fire Watchers on the Town Hall, probably 1944.
Although they lack uniforms – only Fire Guard officers were uniformed – this group of library staff have issue axes, armbands and the grey-painted "Civilian Protective Helmet".
The group have been identified as: Standing, left to right, Mr. Fay, Mr. Langley, Mr. Eggleton and Mr. Johnston: and seated, left to right, Miss Minnie M. Swadling (Deputy Borough Librarian), Pam Reeves, Gloria Lambden, and Joan Budds.
(Reading Libraries 1267503)

In Reading, its committee, working from an office in the ARP area Headquarters in Market Place, had responsibility for

A. Hospital supply and assistants, Transport, two Hospital supply depots

> Central – St Mary's Church House

> Little Dartmouth West Wood Lane

B. Civil Nursing Service – The WVS kept a register for volunteer Civil Nursing

Early Closing Day

Reserve. Trained nurses, members of the Hospital Auxiliary Scheme

WVS mobile canteens supported ARP services and victims at the scene of any raid, and in Reading were amongst the first services on site and last to leave from the People's Pantry bombing in 1943, where members were included amongst the fatalities.

This close integration is illustrated by an Emergency and Invasion Committee minute from 20th September 1943 recording the payment £9/18 to the WVS for

Supplies of tea, sugar and tinned milk for distribution to group points of the Air Raid Wardens service [and for WVS use] in cooperation with the Wardens and Fire Guards for the provision of hot drinks for homeless persons during air raids.

WVS Mobile canteen, c.1940-41.
It isn't certain that this is one of the "Ford Food Vans" used by the Women's Voluntary Service to supply rescue workers following the bombing of 10th February 1943, but it seems likely that this is seen here, again with the Mayor centre stage. The vehicle was presented by nurses from Reading.
(Reading Libraries 1291361)

Conclusion

Clearly considerable effort and expense were put into the development of the infrastructure needed to deal with anticipated air raids of a scale beyond those that actually materialised.

The actual numbers involved go considerably beyond a peak of c.1800-2000 wardens and other directly employed civil defence personnel. For example, each of the three Starfish sites protecting Reading had a "crew" of around twenty men. More importantly, every adult not otherwise engaged in some form of civil defence or Home Guard activity, was brought into nightly fire watching or Fire Guard shifts.

Elsewhere in the country, some ARP services performed excellently, some were overwhelmed and it is important to note that no aid raid on the predicted scale was ever experienced by the UK, including Reading. What is striking is the serious minded diligence with which all levels of precaution were undertaken at an official level. Also, when actually tested – particularly by incendiary raids on Caversham and by the fatal raid of February 1943 - Reading's precautions seem to have paid off, with the structures and individual services generally delivering what had been asked of them.

However, it must be stressed that all raids on Reading were of a very small nature. It is impossible to say if the town's ARP services would have worked against the scale of threat predicted, or against the scale of raid delivered against, for example Birmingham or Liverpool. [130]

The next chapter will show something of the reaction of Reading's ARP services to attack, and give details of all known air raids on the area.[131]

Early Closing Day

Chapter One Notes

1. Margaret Simons WEA Course notes, 2010.
2. *Fighting with Figures*, HMSO, 1995. Table 12.3
3. Civil Defence Emergency Committee Minutes for 1/9/39 (BRO R/AC2/20/1a – cited hereafter as "Committee Minutes")
4. Collier, B (1957) p.77 (See Bibliography)
5. Overy, R (2013), p.49 SEE bibliography.
6. From *Measures necessary after heavy air attack June 1942.* National Archives HO186/931
7. See Mike Cooper and Ray Parkes *We Cannot Park on Both sides.* Reading, 1999 for accounts from these volunteers.
8. Committee minutes 4th May 1945
9. *Fighting with Figures*, HMSO, 1995
10. *Measures necessary* op.cit
11. Berkshire County Control Centre Siren and Incident Log Berkshire Record Office C/D/2/1
12. ibid
13. Berkshire Record Office. *Records of Civil Defence and Emergency Planning: Berkshire County Council.* Undated finding guide.
14. *Pocket Guide to the ARP arrangements in Reading* in Berkshire Record Office (BRO) D/EX1650/1
15. Ibid and Committee Minutes for 2/9/39
16. Return in National Archives HO186/474
17. Committee minutes, op.cit
18. Committee minutes for 4/9/and 12/9/39 BRO R/AC2/20/1a
19. *Pocket Guide to ARP Arrangements* p5
20. Committee minutes 20 Oct 1939
21. ibid
22. Committee minutes for 5th and 20th June 1941 and 25th July 1941
23. Ibid. 8th May 1942
24. The main sources for this section are a series of reports by Colin Dobinson for the Council for British Archaeology. *Twentieth Century Fortifications in England* (1996) Anti Aircraft Artillery is covered in Volumes 1.3 and 1.4. Searchlights are dealt with in Appendix AA/1 (2000). Details of organisation nad Starfish Sites come from Dobinson's books AA Command (Methuen, 2000) and Fields of Deception (Methuen, 2000)
25. Overy, op.cit. p.100
26. Discussion on the "Old Reading" forum on Facebook, 2015. Last accessed 23/01/2016 and notes in Patricia Rolt Christ the King Parish from 1946-1970 [undated]

27.   Committee Minutes, 14th May 1943 and *Home Guard List* for September 1942. Home Guard enrolment is from the Minutes for 13th May 1942.

28.   Hylton, 2007 pp.213-214.

29.   *Reading Mercury* 30th September 1939. Accessed online on 25/2/2016

30.   *Pocket Guide to ARP arrangements* op.cit. p.25.

31.   Caption to Reading Museum object number REDMG : 1980.36.A297.8. Accessed online on 20/02/2016

32.   *Pocket Guide*, Op cit

33.   Committee minutes. 12 December 1939

34.   Ibid, 22nd January 1940

35.   Ibid 2/9/1939

36.   Ibid, 30/10/1940

37.   Ibid, 10th December 1941 and 2nd January 1942.

38.   Discussed in Baker *Enterprise versus bureaucracy* – SEE bibliography.

39.   Berkshire Chronicle, 6th December 1940 quoted in Pentland, R *Put that light out.*

40.   For further comparison of shelter policies and practice SEE Baker, op.cit. Richard Overy *The Bombing war* and Zaloga *Defence of the Third Reich* Osprey, 2012, http://www.military-history.org/articles/air-raid-shelters.htm and https://en.wikipedia.org/wiki/Air-raid_shelter accessed on 14/10/2015

41.   Minutes of 7th August and 30th September 1940,

42.   Op Cit, 11th October

43.   From *Reading County Borough Deep Shelter Scheme church End Quarry, Caversham.* National Archives HO207/1051. The rest of this section draws on correspondence in this file.

44.   Borough Surveyor to Regional Technical Adviser, 9th January 1941, in H) 207/1051 op.cit.

45.   https://en.wikipedia.org/wiki/John_Anderson,_1st_Viscount_Waverley accessed on 16/10/2015

46.   Op cit, page 34.

47.   Committee Minutes, 1st September 1939. For a summary of the development of the shelter see https://facultystaff.richmond.edu/~wgreen/ECDandersonsh.html

48.   Committee minutes 1st, 9th and 26th February 1940

49.   Sixth Report of the Emergency Committee for Civil Defence, presented on 4th February 1940

50.   Committee Minutes, April 14th 1943

51.   Ibid., 16th March 1942

52.   Ibid, 14th July 1944.

53.   For those seeking more on the Warden's service, See Rebecca Puntland's

Early Closing Day

dissertation in the bibliography.

54.   *Pocket Guide to ARP arrangements*

55.   HO186/474

56.   HO186/932

57.   HO186/474

58.   Committee minutes 15th August 1941

59.   Emergency Committee Minutes, 29th September 1939,

60.   Op cit 27 Oct 1941

61.   Diary/Log Book of post in Records of Chief ARP Warden 1939-1958
(Berkshire Records Office D/EX1657/1-6)

62.   Op Cit, p.6

63.   Committee Minutes 14th September 1939

64.   Ibid, 6 December 1939

65.   Ibid, 23rd October 1940

66.   Ibid 19th August 1943

67.   Ibid.

68.   Ibid 1st September 1939 and 28th Sept 1939

69.   In BRO at DEX1657/1

70.   Committee Minutes 10th October 1039

71.   Ibid 30th September 1943

72.   Ibid, 15th December 1939

73.   Ibid.

74.   Pocket Guide to ARP, p.43

75.   Ibid, 4th September 1939

76.   *Pocket Guide to ARP*, p.6

77.   *Reading Mercury* 23rd September 1939. Accessed via National Newspaper
Library online on 20th February 2016

78.   Committee Minutes 21st March 1947

79.   Ibid.13th November 1939 and 4th November 1942.

80.   For more on this, and the role of Reading Corporation Transport in ARP, see
Ray Smith and John Whitehead *War and Austerity*...Milane, 2014.

81.   DEX 1657/1 op cit.

82.   Committee Minutes 21st and 27th February and 5th March 1940, and 30 th
June and 29#8th July 1941

83.   *Reading Mercury* 16th December 1939. Accessed only on 20th February 2016

84.   Dave Doe, *Flames over the Valley* (Reading: The Author, [undated , 2016]
pp.209

85.   There is no history of Reading's Police in WW2, and the standard work A.
Wylkes *The Queens Peace...(*Reading Corporation, 1968) gives very little detail.
http://www.thamesvalley.police.uk/museum_booklet_a4.pdf has some
information about all the Forces which made up Thames Valley Police.

86.   *Pocket Guide to ARP*, op.cit.

87.   Reading Corporation. Watch Committee Minutes 16th February 1943 at Berkshire Records Office AC1/3/97

88.   *Home Guard List*, September 1941.

89.   *Home Guard List*, 1942 and Committee minutes 13th may 1942

90.   Committee Minutes 21st May 1943

91.   Ibid. 2nd September 1942 and in the Wardens post log referred to in note liv above.

92.   Ibid, 21st April 1943

93.   HO186/474 War Establishment of No6 Region, Reading

94.   ibid

95.   *Pocket Guide to the ARP Arrangements in Reading* op. cit. and Committee Minutes at BRO R/AC2/20/1a

96.   Ibid

97   As mentioned in the text a key source here is Alan Sandall's *Are you 17* (Frome: The Author, 1991). National level information is taken from sources given in the Bibliography, with the addition of House, Alan *Wheels of Fire…* (Southampton: Housefire books, 2010). Dave Doe's *Flames in the Valley*: *Berkshire Fire Fighters 1700-1960* Reading: The Author [Un dated – 2016] provides a lot of detail, bit still relatively little on the War years, and is largely without citation of sources.

98.   Ibid.

99.   Quoted, but without a source in Doe pp.189 – see note 97 above

100. Ibid pp.207.

101. Sandall (1991) pp.86

102. Drury, Colin *Terror Raid Reading*, 2013

103. Sandall op. cit pp.114-145, 166

104. Committee Minutes 21st April 1943

105. Doe, *Flames over the Valley*, op. cit.

106. Ibid pp.209.

107. Minutes 6th April 1943

108. Ibid 22nd September 1943.

109. Ibid 19th July 1943

110. Ibid. 8th September 1944

111. Ibid 25th February 1943

112. Measures necessary… Op cit, p.7

113. Committee Minutes 6th September 1939.

114. Ibid.

115. Drury, Colin. *Terror Raid Reading*, 2013

116. Measures necessary op. cit

117. For details of these kitchens see Lynda Chater, Food shortages and

Early Closing Day

rationing in the Reading area. In *Berkshire in the First World War*. (Reading: Reading Libraries, 2015) pp.85-96

118.   Minutes, 28th May 1941

119.   Ibid, 8th May 1942

120.   Women's Voluntary Service for Civil Defence Monthly Narrative Report, Reading Centre March 1943. Also online at https://wrvslearning.wordpress.com/activities/bombing/

121.   Reading Corporation Housing Committee Minutes at Berkshire Record Office AC1/3/97

122.   *Berkshire Chronicle* 19th December 1941. Accessed via http://collections.readingmuseum.org.uk/index.asp?page=record&mwsquery=%7Btotopic%7D=%7BWomen%20in%20the%20Second%20World%20War%7D&filename=REDMG&hitsStart=31

123.   *Measures necessary*, op cit.

124.   After Raid Report and WVS monthly narrative op. cit.

125.   Minutes, 29th May 1943

126.   Ibid.

127.   *Measures Necessary*, Op.cit

128.   Berkshire Civil Defence Committee minutes op, cit 5th February 1945

129.   For a more detailed treatment see Robert and Patricia Malcomson *Women at the Ready...* Abacus, 2014

A *Berkshire Chronicle* photo showing people reacting to the first air raid warning of the War. On 6th September 1939, an alert was sounded at 7.32am with the all clear at 9.02. Reading Museum REDMG : 1980.36.A297.8. Copyright Reading Museum (Reading Borough Council. All rights reserved).

Chapter 2
The "Blitz" - 1940 - 1941
Bombs on Reading

This chapter attempts to detail every air attack on Reading from June 1940 to May 1941 given in primary sources available at the time of writing.

Although the fatal raid in February 1943 is most remembered, most bombs that fell on Reading in the Second World War were dropped during this period – around 60 high explosive bombs and at least 400 individual incendiary bombs.

The Blitz

In British historiography it is usual to describe this period as "The Battle of Britain" and "The Blitz", with the former starting just after the evacuation of British forces from Dunkirk and Calais in June 1940, and the latter marking the German Air Force's - the Luftwaffe's - switch to city targets from September 1940 until May 1941. However, it has been noted that this is a British distinction, not one made by the Luftwaffe, who treated both these periods as one campaign.

At the time of writing it has not been possible to determine the reasons why any given attack on Reading occurred. However, German strategic aims during the period are well enough understood so that, whilst it is not possible to answer a question such as "So why was my house bombed?", it is possible to look at what the Luftwaffe was attempting to achieve overall at this time.

Meeting in August 1940, the Berkshire County Council Civil Defence Committee – with responsibility outside Reading – heard that the British Ministry of Home Security considered that German objectives for any bombing would be -

A. Shipping and ports

B. Industrial areas so as to reduce production

C. Areas containing aggregations of population the bombing of which might be calculated to produce panic

D. Aerodromes[1]

As far as can be told, at no time was Reading attacked by more than one aircraft. Most German raids on the U.K. during 1940 and 1941 were nuisance attacks – "Storangriffe". Of around 5200 individual raids logged in German war diaries, only 171 were major attacks.[2]

The aim of these attacks was to test defences, give crews training and gather information, as well as to keep the British on edge, attacking morale. In addition to these missions, prisoner interrogation showed that German crews were briefed to bomb any lights visible as targets of opportunity.[3]

Early Closing Day

In summer 1940 the Luftwaffe attempted to strike against airfields to gain air superiority ahead of any landing in Britain, but, alongside this, flew attacks against industrial targets with the intention of forcing Britain to negotiate for surrender. "The Blitz" saw these attacks delivered by night, as losses in summer 1940 had shown that it was not viable to operate bombers over the UK by day. The majority of the attacks on Reading came in the hours of darkness over the winter months.

By 1941, Reading appeared on a Luftwaffe target list, as a second order target for attacks on the aircraft industry, ranking next to last on the list.[4]

In Chapter 1 it was stated that the degree of devastation forecast before the war was beyond the Germans means to deliver. This does not mean that the Luftwaffe did not pose a meaningful threat to Reading – or rather, could not have done so had it so chosen. Cities across the United Kingdom were badly bombed, virtually at will in the face of weak night time defences, killing around 40,000 people and destroying thousands of buildings. However, even this was not on the scale of damage inflicted by Allied bombing on Germany or Japan.

In 1940 the Luftwaffe's bomber strength committed to the attack on the United Kingdom stood at 764. Of these 484 were actually serviceable and hence available at the start of the Blitz.[5] In practice this meant that up to around 150-350 aircraft would be put over a given target on a given night – the highest total actually achieved during the period was 712 over London on April 19th 1941 (although this may have included multiple sorties by individual aircraft).

With the Junkers Ju88 only just appearing in significant numbers, this force consisted of two types, the Heinkel He111 family and the Dornier Do17 family.

Both were designs approaching obsolescence, and neither was capable of the range with a bombload to allow strategic bombing of the type practised by the British and Americans. The aircraft were intended primarily for use in support of the army, on targets such as troop concentrations, railways installations and defences.

Over Britain, their chief limitations by night were range, bomb load and the ability to find and bomb a target by night with a sufficiently concentrated load of bombs to cause severe and lasting destruction.

The 712 aircraft bombing London on April 19th 1941 dropped just over 1000tons of high explosive bombs and more than 4200 clusters of incendiaries. This exceeded pre-war estimates, but it was a quite exceptional "high" over a target available at quite short range, and yet still represented under two tons of bombs per bomber. Attacks on targets further from their bases in France saw tonnages drop to around a ton per aircraft. A raid on Plymouth in January 1941 delivered around half a ton of high explosive bombs per aircraft.

The highest weight of bombs delivered on any target in the Reading area was probably 4000kg (8800lbs or just over 3.5tons) - four bombs on Woodley, of which the only one recovered was of 1000kg - this does not mean the entire load was of this weight. Much more representative of the load that the Luftwaffe could deliver in 1940 was the 990lbs (0.4 tons) of high explosive bombs dropped on Caversham in October 1940.

Table 1, below summarises the known information about bombs dropped on Reading

Year	High Explosive (number of bombs)	High Explosive Bombs (approx. weight)	Incendiaries	Buildings damaged (approx)	Known casualties
1940	94	4950lb known - probably c. 80-90 110lb bombs	Unknown - but stated to have been dropped.	At least 16	3
1941	12		350+	At least 8	8
1942	2				
1943	4	4400lb		At least 6 severely damaged	41 fatal, 51 serious.
1944	1	1870lb		At least 2	4
Total	113	Identified weight = 11220lb/ c.4.6tons includ- ing one V1 Flying Bomb warhead	350+	At least 32	41 fatal, 51 serious over 100 others

11,00lbs – and that is only an approximation from securely identified bombs in ARP records – represents approximately the bomb load of a single RAF Avro Lancaster.

At this time most high explosive German bombs were what the RAF would describe as "General Purpose" with under half their weight comprising high explosive filling, but with steel cases strong enough to allow them to withstand impact with a target before exploding. Increasingly, during 1940 and 1941 the

Early Closing Day

Luftwaffe began to drop clusters of small incendiary bombs intended solely to cause fires in buildings as well as high explosive bombs. As an example, in one night in December 1940 Liverpool received around 900 such clusters, perhaps in the order of 32,000 individual small bombs.[6]

Dusseldorf, Reading's twin town in Germany, was attacked by the RAF a number of times between 1942 and 1944, receiving over 18,000 tons of bombs of all types.[7]

It is also worth questioning if the idea of Reading as the actual target of the attacks described here is valid. Certainly Reading was bombed, but without better information from the German side, there is no certainty that it was Reading that was the known and intentional target.

In 1940 – indeed throughout the Second World War – night-time bombing accuracy was very low. Both sides struggled to find their specified targets and to hit them when they found them. "Hits" in this context might mean little more than bombs dropped approximately in the urban area of a target town.

Although the Luftwaffe benefitted from some sophisticated navigational aids even these might not allow an attack to be more precise than on a given area of a given target. The bombing of Coventry on 14th November 1940 was remarkably accurate, largely hitting the industrial area (and its surrounding residential areas) but this was the product of skilled bombing using the then state-of the art "Y Gerat" system, otherwise known as "Wotan", to allow individual "pathfinder" aircraft to be controlled by ground stations and instructed when to bomb. Y Gerat and its predecessors were most unlikely to have been used by the individual aircraft bombing Reading, and, in any case, all were subject, eventually, to British counter measures.[8]

Once over the target area, a German bomber did not release one bomb on one location and move off, it dropped its entire load in a "stick" some of which might actually hit where the bomb aimer had intended, but most of which would fall over a wider area depending on variables including the bombers height above the ground and speed. One attack on Caversham left bombs (including incendiaries) from Salisbury Road, south of the Thames up into Peppard Road, spreading along at least two miles.

The first recorded attack in the general area of Reading was on July 3rd 1940, with a single bomb on Aldermaston; the last on 19th March 1945 happened when a V2 missile exploded over Cockpole Green near Wargarve.[9] For the purposes of this chapter, "Reading" will be defined as the area covered by Reading

Corporation, with the addition of Woodley. Inevitably, this puts raids logged by the Berkshire County ARP network out of reach – Shinfield, Winnersh, Theale, Arborfield and Three Mile Cross, for example, were all bombed in 1940. Excluding these areas partly reflects a lack of detail in the Berkshire reports, but is largely a reaction to space and time constraints.

Caversham

From the reports presented at the time, Caversham was raided four times in 1940-41, taking a total of twenty six high explosive (HE) bombs and over 300 incendiaries. Machine gun fire from the raid on the town centre on 10th February 1943 hit Caversham, and this is dealt with in Chapter 3.

All four raids would have been delivered either in darkness or at dusk.

The details given below are quoted from the senior ARP officer's reports, given verbatim except where the original text requires clarification. These reports were written by a man who knew what he was referring to, for people who could be expected to share his understanding, not a modern audience! At seventy five years distance, they can be terse and, in some instances, vague and confusing.

1st October 1940

05.00 – Nine 110lb HE bombs fell [10] across Caversham -

1. Rumbles Allotment/Old Sewage Works at rear of Star Road

2. Open ground in Woodlands Farm off Lower Henley Road

3. Centre of Upper Henley Rd. at the junction with Anglefield Rd. Damage to houses each side of the road

4. Front drive between numbers 14 and 15 Pembroke Place, damaging houses and leaving crater

5. In back gardens of 12 and 13 Pembroke Place damaging both houses

6. Allotments at rear and NE side of Chiltern Road

7. As 6

8. In field S of Oratory School

9. Open ground beside swimming baths of Oratory School

Early Closing Day

It is not clear from the log account if this was the actual order in which the bombs fell. In general the wardens seem to have made an effort to establish the sequence of events as accurately as possible, and the Anglefield Road bomb was certainly *reported* before those at Pembroke Place. The assumption here will be that in each of the reports given the first bomb referred to was the first to fall.

Wardens' Post A5 (in Darell Road) reported gas and electricity mains damaged with police and utilities on the scene.

At 06.10 ARP Post A12 (Holloway's Garage, Henley Road) rang the Control Centre and reported damage at the junction of Henley and Anglefield Road,

The crater in the centre of Henley Road at the junction was roped off.

Ten minutes later Post A11 (Electricity Sub-Station, Chiltern Road) reported damage to Pembroke Place, with one case of shock at numbers 14 and 15.

The following day, T. Hubbard, Head Warden for A Group, reported on the incident to the Chief Warden, Ronald Ruston. Oddly, his reports give the times shown above which, if the "05.00" given in the summary report is accurate, must have been after initial assessments were made.

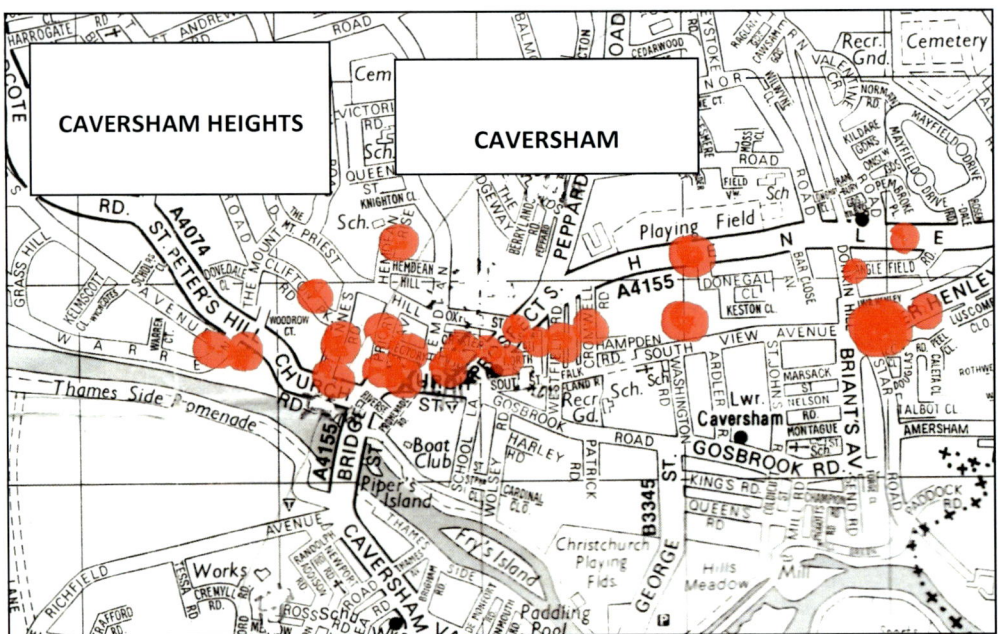

The Head Warden's report noted -

Position of the Henley Rd Anglefield Rd incident was discovered by Messenger Collings of Post A12 who cycled into the crater...The lad bruised his wrist....

(All Wardens posts had young messengers attached to them, often Boy Scouts.

Messenger Collings was later awarded eight shillings compensation for damage to his bike).

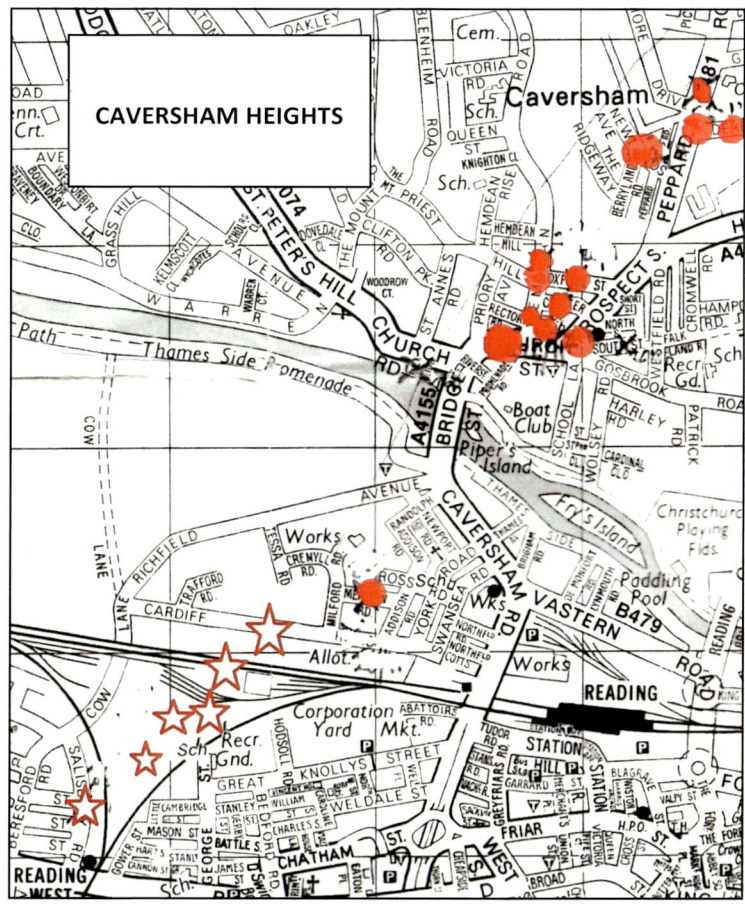

Sketch maps (above and opposite) showing the fall of bombs on Caversham during the raids of 26th November 1940 (above), and 30th January 1941. High Explosive bombs are marked with a star, incendiary bombs with a dot. Note that the locations are approximate only and are taken from the contemporary Wardens' reports.

Early Closing Day

"Antsnest" a correspondent on the Reading Forum remembered this incident, writing in 2011:

I remember the bomb at Henley Rd - Anglefield Rd, it dropped right outside our house! The steel framed windows were bowed right in, and there was a photo in the local paper of a team of firemen pulling them straight again. The roof was removed and a large hole was blown through the wall separating the two front bedrooms. Part of the bomb casing left a long dent in the lamp post outside the house (is the same one still there?), and we later found many pieces of the bomb casing in the garden, which made good 'swapsies' at school. The only casualty was a cyclist, who pedalled into the crater in the blackout. Fortunately, my mum and I happened to be staying with my gran that night. [12]

The two bombs that fell near the Oratory School were remembered by a former pupil, David Rowney. [13]

We were all in bed when the first bomb dropped. It seemed so close and shook all the windows, though all we were worried about was that it might have landed on the cricket square. The plane droned overhead and dropped another bomb which landed on the changing room for the outside swimming pool. By this time we were all out of bed and scrambling to get downstairs to the cellars where there were bunks. The plane went on and the air raid siren sounded the all clear. I remember hoping that the pool itself might have been damaged, since swimming outdoors in cold water was not my favourite activity, but no such luck!

The "110lb HE" referred in the ARP reports were almost certainly the standard German SC50, the most common bomb used during this period. As this raid shows, most German bombers could carry eight to ten giving an all up load of around 1000-2000lbs at longer range. An experiment carried out for the Channel 4 television programme *Blitz Street* showed that a replica SC50 was quite capable of demolishing a terraced house with a direct hit. [14] As discussed above, it is highly unlikely any individual buildings could have been targeted that morning.

9th October 1940

05.35 – 4 HE bombs plus 6 outside the Borough Boundary. No casualties, no damage logged

> 256 Peppard Rd
>
> Hedge on drive leading to St B?? Home, Kidmore End Road

Garden St Beat?? Home

Garden 58 Kidmore End Rd

The name of the home concerned is illegible in the original text, but was probably St Benet's, a home for boys run by the Children's Society at number 11 Kidmore End Rd. Opened as a school and agricultural training centre, in 1905, St Benet's became a residential home in 1921, closing in 1980.[15]

No details are given of the six bombs that fell over the Reading boundary, and no trace of records from Oxfordshire has been found at the time of writing.

The number of bombs suggests that these were at most 110lb SC50s.

26th November 1940

19.55 - Seven 110lb HE plus "numerous" incendiaries

West Side of Cardiff Road opposite "Wymans" causing "severe" damage to 79 and 81, with lesser damage to 75, 77 and 83.

Garden of 69 Salisbury Rd

Near Reading West Loop

Loco Yard

Through hard water tank adjoining loco sheds

Between up and down lines 40-50 yards west of "West Goods Box". Lifted two wagons off tracks from passing trains. The Great Western Railway (GWR) ARP service reported the line broken between Tilehurst and Reading and a UXB 300 yards west of Caversham Road.

Pole Yard on N side of West Goods Box

Incendiaries

53-55 Church St

5, 7 and 16 Hemdean Rd

Meadow Rd

6 Oxford St

Caversham Library

Chester St

Early Closing Day

GWR Signal Offices

Oratory School Grounds – 2 bombs

135 Peppard Rd

Regal Cinema grounds – 3 bombs

House Close

Newlands Avenue – in woods

Buckside

12 South St – garden

The incendiaries dropped were almost certainly the one kilogramme B1El, with a magnesium case and a filling of Thermite which burns at very high temperatures.   These were dropped in canisters of thirty six, with a single bomber able to carry over a thousand bomblets. By 1941, some bomblets had an explosive charge added to hinder – or directly attack – ARP services.[16]

The spread of the incendiaries produced a range of incident reports, and this bombing, the worst of the "Blitz" period, is very well represented in surviving documents including reports from individual policemen and the Upper Thames Patrol of the Home Guard.

The Cardiff Road bomb caused the most serious incident, with two houses – presumably 79 and 81 - described as "demolished" by in a police report at 20.25. The incident was reported to the Control Room at 19.56 by Post D2 (at Wyman's printing company in Cardiff Road itself), which said that people were trapped, followed by reports that gas and water mains had been damaged, and requests for another rescue party at 20.07 and 20.12. By 20.20 the Reading Gas Company was on site and the main was being dealt with. The immediate work on the incident had finished by ten o'clock.

The actual timing of the incident is generally clear, but it is worth noting that contemporary reports give timings from 19.50, when post C1 (Battle Farm) and A11 (Chiltern Road) reported damage at the rear of 69 Salisbury Road and incendiaries in Chiltern Road respectively, through to 19.54 with Posts A9 (Surley Row) and A2 (Caversham Parochial School) reporting incidents at 19.55 and 19.56.

Given the nature of the events it is not surprising that individual timings vary.

The reports coming into the Report Centre in the Town Hall give a vivid picture of the ARP network working, and also how confused an incident like this could be when many small bombs were spread over a wide area with a number of posts and individuals involved.

Following the original timings given on the message forms, the Report Centre's picture of what was happening developed as follows.

19.45   An unknown caller – probably a Policeman - contacts the Police to report *I was in my workroom at 2 George St Reading when I heard a "whizz" but no explosion...*

19.50   Post C1 (Beresford Road) reports damage in Salisbury Road

19.54   Constable Leadbetter (No.91) reports *I was at the junction of Waverley-Wantage Roads when I heard 2 bombs whistle and I believe they were near the Railway line at the bottom of Little Johns Lane. Aircraft overhead at the time.*

19.55   Post A2 (School Lane, Caversham) reports a fire in Caversham Park off Peppard Rd – bushes and the common are on fire.

Post C5   (Grovelands School) reports 3-4 explosions...whistling bombs and incendiaries

Bombed houses in Cardiff Road, November 1940.
These are 79 and 81, hit by a single 110lb bomb in the evening of 26th November 1940.
The same raid also hit Salisbury Road and put bombs over the railway and a scatter of incendiaries across Caversham.
(Reading Libraries 1336398)

Early Closing Day

19.56   Post D2 in Cardiff Road makes its report

                 A2 reports an incendiary bomb

19.58   A2 reports a fire at the junction of Hemdean Road and Priest Hill

An unidentified caller reports a fire in Hemdean Road, but won't say more.

Post A9   (Surley Row, Caversham) reports a fire in the grounds of the Oratory School.

Post A2   reports an incendiary and a fire at the bottom of Prospect St.

Constable Jupp (No.42) reports *I was in Derby Road a few minutes ago when an incendiary bomb fell ten yards away. I obtained a shovel and put it out. I also put out two more in Derby Road and one in Peppard Road at the corner of Derby Road. I made enquiries of the residents in the vicinity and was informed that they had put out several more. There does not appear to be any more in the vicinity.* (PC Rex Jupp was killed by the bomb that destroyed the People's Pantry in 1943).

Post A11   (Chiltern Rd) reports an incident at the top left hand side of Chiltern Road. Incendiary bombs have been extinguished, but they aren't clear if there are any unexploded bombs.

Post D2   reports that gas and water mains in Cardiff Road have been damaged.

Special Constable No.208 reports that an incendiary bomb in House Close has been dealt with by "wardens and self".

Post A9 says the fires in the Oratory School grounds are out.

Post D2 asks for another rescue party for Cardiff Road

20.15   Post C5 reports HE and incendiary bombs have fallen North of Town between the Pond House and Caversham Bridge across the Warren

20.25   Inspector Bryant reports that two houses have been destroyed in Cardiff Road. "Persons" have been rescued, and there are casualties, but gas is escaping and the water main is broken.

20.27   The Home Guard's Upper Thames Patrol, Section 4, Stretch B, reports incendiaries North West of Caversham Bridge

By half past eight the police had established an incident post at number 16 Hemdean Road, and were able to report that "sufficient" fire appliances were in attendance. Just under an hour and a half later Cardiff Road had been roped off, the gas company had disconnected the supply to the damaged houses, the road repair gang which had attended the incident had been sent back to their depot until daylight and accommodation had been found for those made homeless.

The UXB – Unexploded Bomb – on the railway was almost certainly an SC50, The SC50 could not generally contain a time fuse, and so if one was found unexploded standard practice would be to blow it up in situ, or to treat it as reasonably safe and move it away for disposal. One puzzling feature is the UXB referred to by Post A1. Nothing is mentioned in the summary report, and if the Chiltern Road UXB was a genuine incident, it is hard to see how it can have been an SC50.

One of the two incendiaries to fall in the grounds of the Oratory School was mentioned in the School Magazine in 1941. [17]

Since the beginning of the Michaelmas Term 1940, the boys have been sleeping in the cellars. These have been fitted with bunks with spring mattresses for each boy; they are heated by the hot water system and fitted with electric light. No adverse effects have been observed on the health or spirits of the boys. A fire-fighting service had been organized by Mr Sempill, but so far have only had to cope with one incendiary bomb in a remote part of the woods.

In *Roots and Branches* David Cliffe records the experience of a boy who encountered incendiaries later that day when he cycled to renew his library books.

Having watched people collecting sandbags to extinguish bombs which had fallen in Hemdean Road and Chester Street, he reached the library only to be told: *Go away boy, we've got bombs on the roof...*[18]

In Hemdean Road, Ron Atkins' grandparents' house was hit.[19] *My grandparents in Hemdean Road had one which went through the roof and into their bedroom. A warden smothered it with sand and put it out but it left a nasty black hole in the ceiling*

The Group report to the Chief Warden later that day stated that Post Warden Page (of D2), Deputy Post Warden Miss Wheeler, Warden Wheeler and another warden, whose name is illegible, were in the post at the time. They would have been just across the road from the first or second bomb to fall. They sent out a patrol, picking up Warden Harland on the way and checked for casualties.

The four occupants of 83 Cardiff Road (owned by Ernest Coward) and the sole

Early Closing Day

occupants of 79 and 81, were found safe. Those in number 75 (listed in 1942 as being owned by a Mrs M Proctor) were found to be "very nervous" and moved to friends in Prospect Street.

The only Civil Defence casualty was Warden Moon (whose post is not stated, but was probably D2), who was bruised by the blast of the bomb. Warden Moon was treated at the Caversham First Aid Post in the Parochial School in School Lane. It is probably Warden Moon who is referred to in a message to the control room from D2 at 23.15 stating that someone – the name is illegible – had reported back from the First Aid Post badly bruised.

The wardens stopped traffic, and, due to the ruptured gas main, warned the occupants of the nearest houses to put out any fires, also warning bystanders to stop smoking.

Post C1 (Battle Farm/Beresford Rd) gave a snapshot of what one 110lb SC50 could do after investigating the one which fell at the back of 69 Salisbury Road. J.W.H Perrin, the Head Warden went to the scene and reported that the bomb caused slight damage to numbers 67 and 69, leaving a 14ft diameter crater.

If the sequence of events reported in the original document is accurate, the main aiming point for the Germans seems to have been the railway. The triangle of lines, just north of Reading West Station, shows up clearly on a Luftwaffe photograph believed to be from 1940 – and indeed was marked as a railway junction.[20] Given this, then, flying approximately South West to North East across Reading, the aircraft effectively straddled the railway with SC50s, unloading at least one incendiary cluster over the built up area of Caversham, and it seems reasonable to assume that this was what was being aimed at.

Six of the eight high explosive bombs certainly hit the railway line and related buildings.

The report given to the Emergency Committee for Civil Defence said that he wardens of Post D2 at the centre of the worst incident that night had attended to their duties in a most efficient manner.

30th January 1941

16.35 – c. 300 incendiaries in the area from St Peter's Avenue to the "Borough Boundary". Eight casualties and small fires with damage to fifty six properties.

The extent of the raid meant that the ARP services had to estimate the numbers of small bombs involved in this attack. Those reported were:

On buildings

St Peters Church	1
Bayliss, Church St	1
10, 11, 17 and 28 Rectory Rd	4
14, 15, 28 St Anne's Rd	3
Priory Avenue, corner of Church St	1
18 Priory Avenue	1
Hemdean Rd adjoining Library	1
5 Hemdean Rise	1
Shed at corner of Prospect St and Chester St	1
Corner of North St	1
East end of Short St	1
17 and 21 Westfield Rd	2
5 and 58 Cromwell Rd	2
248 and 256 Henley Rd	2
71 and 94 Lower Henley Road (shed)	2

On roads or open ground

Junction St Peter's Avenue and the Warren	9 bombs
St Peter's Churchyard	11
Garden of no 31 Church Rd	3
Numbers 3 and 5 Church Road	3 with 2 in a shed
Gardens of numbers 6, 10,14, 15, 17, 27, 28, 36 and 38 St Anne's Road	Estimated at 12
7 and 14 Clifton Park Road	2
Clifton Park Road	2
10 Rectory Road	2
Rectory Rd	Estimated 6

Early Closing Day

24 Prospect St	3
Junction of Hemdean Rd and Church Rd	9
South View Avenue Recreation Ground	2
[Illegible] in road	4 + 2
Star Road, Junction of Donkin Hill "East Of Star House"	
	Estimate 50

Others fell outside the Borough Boundary.

Fires were started in Prospect Street - in a house and a shop, Chester Street – in a small furniture store - Cromwell Road, Lower Henley Road, St Anne's Road, Henley Road and Anglefield Road.

Church Street Caversham, 1930s.
Church Street may possibly claim to have taken more individual bombs – all small incendiaries – than any other street in Reading. The Library, and just across the road, the Regal Cinema were hit or subject to near misses November 1940 and January 1941. Next door to the Library is the Caversham Electric Theatre, later the Glendale.
(Reading Libraries 1225674)

The Auxiliary Fire Service (AFS)– including that from Caversham, based at Caversham Court, Henley and No2 Unit from Tilehurst - worked to control the fires, and only the bombs that fell on Cromwell Road seem to have started enough of a fire to be described as "taking hold" at 16.37 by the wardens of post A2 (Caversham Parochial School).

The caretaker of the Recreation Ground in South View Avenue put two bombs out and the AFS put out a bomb on St Peter's Church – possibly just making it safe as it was not found until nine o'clock. Mr Stratton of 214 Henley Road was reported to have had an incendiary in a bucket in his garden. In Hemdean Road, next to the Library, Warden Dunster broke into a house where the owner was out and put out another bomb.

Eight people were injured, four of whom required hospital treatment, although one only as an out-patient.

Despite the widespread nature of the incident – more properties were damaged than in any other raid on the town - it appears from the log of reports to the control room that most, if not all, of the fires were out or on their way to being out by 17.20 when Auxiliary Fire Service units and rescue parties were reported as returning to depot. At 17.31 the Chief Constable told Reading Control "All fires out".

The number of incendiaries need only represent a single large cluster, but more probably represent more than one. Wardens at post A5 (Darrell Road) said that they had found "what appears to be a piece of an aeroplane" at 8 Albert Road. The Post Warden of A12 (Henley Road) took what he described as "Four IB [Incendiary Bomb] holders and several fins" to the police, suggesting that at least four clusters were dropped, with perhaps a fifth falling in Albert Road. If a cluster was usually 36 bomblets, this would give approaching 200 incendiaries.

Writing for the History of Reading Society in 2015, Robin Gardner, who lived in Church Road, recalled that evening:

One of the bombs hit the roof [of his home] on the street side, it did not penetrate the roof but slid down and landed on the front door step, where Dad put out the fire, and brought the steaming offending item up to show us in a bucket of water. When he got down, someone had pinched the tail fin, much to Dad's disgust, it was "our bomb! [21]

Reading - Coley.

The Coley area was the first part of Reading itself to be bombed, with the area from Coley Park to Tilehurst Road being hit three times in 1940-41.

Early Closing Day

3rd October, 05.10 – 4 small HE bombs dropped from Castle Crescent to waste ground opposite Coley Baths. The Berkshire Record Office files show both the involvement of the ARP services, and the confusion in detail that could occur early in an incident.

1. On pavement opposite St Saviour's Church Hall, damaging the Hall, rear of four cottages in St Saviours Road and two houses in Wolseley St. A coffee stall next door to the Hall was burnt out and the Post Warden from Post E6 (Coley Recreation Ground) evacuated thirty five people who had been sheltering in the Hall via the emergency exit. The Post Warden at post E3 (Wolesley St) noted the time of the bomb as 05.30 and stated that it was an incendiary. A milkman's horse was hit and one casualty was caused at 10 Dover St. Post E4 (3 Castle Crescent) reported two HE bombs at 05.20, and that one of its wardens had passed the spot on his way to the post a few minutes earlier.

2. To the right of number 3 Castle Crescent, causing slight damage to the house and the windows and door of Wardens Post E4. The report of the incident stated that the bomb fell three feet from the post. The Post's telephone was taken down, windows broken and the door latch blown off.

3. Rear of 19 Castle Crescent probably causing the one slight casualty reported from 23 Castle Crescent

4. South side of Berkeley Avenue on waste ground near Coley Baths

Post E6 reported five HE bombs dropped at around 05.10. One of their patrols reported the incident at 05.18, and they noted that the fire service were on the scene at 05.25, followed by the Auxiliary Fire Service at 05.50.

In his final report on the incident, the E Group Head Warden (whose signature is eligible, but who is listed as A. E .Negus in the earlier "Pocket Guide")[22] stated that the bombs were "light fragmentation type similar to the 20lb Cooper type used…in the last war"

Arthur Negus, who lived in Franklin Street at the time, went on to be a well known television antiques expert, having risen through the Civil Defence services to oversee training for all fire watchers. The bombs involved here are hard to identify. If Arthur Negus' description is accurate, they would be about 10kg in weight, possibly less. There were a number of small German bombs in this range, but it is hard to pinpoint just which, and the small number involved is strange as smaller bombs tended to be dropped in clusters like incendiaries. The

Chapter 2

larger SC50 would probably have caused more damage. However, at least one of Negus' colleagues was sure the bomb he dealt with was an incendiary.

It is not certain what the target was – if indeed there was a target as such and the German aircraft was not just jettisoning its bombs over a convenient built up area – but it has been suggested that the Coley Branch Line, which ran just south of the fall of bombs, and which was clearly visible on a 1940 German aerial photograph, could have been the aiming point.[23]

In addition to the presence of a local celebrity, this raid is also of interest as one of the only occasions in which it is clear that the air raid warning had sounded and that people had taken shelter.

In her book *Coley: Portrait of an Urban Village*,[24] Phoebe Cusden (formerly Mayor of Reading, and founder of the Reading-Dusseldorf Association) states the school log records on 3rd October 1940 that a bomb was dropped, and on 7th November at 10.15 a bomb exploded. *All children ... were inside the shelters within two and a half minutes.*

The 3rd October incident is clearly that referred to here, but as far as can be ascertained at the time of writing, no bombs fell on Reading on November 7th. In fairness, the account only states that a bomb "exploded". Bombs were dropped on Tidmarsh at 00.10 that morning and at 19.25 on the evening of the 5th November on Tilehurst, leaving six unexploded. The school log may be referring to one of these. [25]

The coffee stall mentioned is remembered as an old railway carriage being run by Alice Wicks, also landlady of the Borough Arms, in Brook Street.[26] Debris from the stall is held by Reading Museum at the time of writing.

Writing on the Reading Forum, "Dids" recalled that her mother, who witnessed the incident, said that -

> *there was a milk float right near where it landed. The milk float was driven by a girl. The horse was hit by shrapnel. Mum said naturally everyone was milling around the girl because she was pretty shaken and no one was seeing to the poor horse.*[27]

In addition to the damage to number 3 Castle Crescent, numbers 4, 6, 8 and 10 were also damaged, with the owner claiming £10/8/8 from the Property Owners War Risks Mutual Society Ltd for "war damage" in the form of broken windows and damaged frames. [28]

Early Closing Day

15th November 1940, 22.45 1 HE on Coley Park Farm. This was technically outside the Borough for ARP purposes and no further details are given in the county ARP records.

9th April 1941 - 22.50 – 50 incendiaries fell in the Tilehurst Road-Berkeley Avenue area causing a minor fire in one house, no casualties.

The report states that the majority of the bombs fell on "swamp ground", with only eight on the residential area. From the location of the bombs that did fall into the residential streets it seems likely that the ground referred to would be that adjacent to the Holy Brook and Kennet and Avon Canal.

First reports were picked up by the wardens in E Group from spotters at "Simonds No 1 Observation Post". The Group was based at the brewery and the firm maintained fire spotters who were also the first to spot the bomber involved in the fatal raid in 1943. Posts E1 and E5 were alerted and those from E1 – at 203 Oxford Road – went to investigate. The exact timing isn't clear from the report, but it seems likely that the bombs were dropped just before eleven o'clock – the earliest time given is 22.50, with the latest 23.12.

The area affected was quite widespread. The locations given in ARP report are:

1. 52 Baker St

2. 33 Coley Avenue – dealt with by a fire watcher

3. 28 Castle Crescent – dealt with by the Auxiliary Fire Service

4. Mansfield Rd

5. Tilehurst Road near the Jolly Brewers pub – two bombs dealt with by Warden Bishop of post E4 (Castle Crescent) and a fire watcher. The bombs "blazed fiercely but were out in three minutes"

6. Junction of Bath Rd and Brunswick St – dealt with by wardens from E5 (Gatehouse Hotel, Bath Road), and reported at 22.57

7. Coley Recreation Ground – extinguished by Head Warden Nash at 22.59 with sand bags. This was later noted to be a high explosive bomb.

8. 21 Boston Avenue

9. "Ministry of Health Grounds" – put out by wardens from E5

10. In field opposite Castle Lodge – this was dealt with by a soldier with a spade and shovel

11. Corporation dump at Manor Farm, Basingstoke Road – reported by Constable Saunders at 23.00

12. Junction of Bartlett's Place and Castle St – reported 23.10 by Post E5

13. North of, or near, Littlecote Drive, Berkeley Avenue – reported by E6 (Coley Recreation Ground) at 23.12

All incidents were dealt with by 23.17.

The post warden of E2, which was on the corner of Soho St and Hope St – both now demolished – wrote an account of how one incendiary was dealt with, showing that the systems set up usually meant someone was on the spot to deal with an incident, but that this wasn't always completely successful.

At about ten to eleven Mrs Saunders (from the context a warden) was walking along Baker Street from Prospect Street and saw an incendiary fall. An airman threw a bucket of water over it, which just seemed to cause it to blaze "furiously". No sand was available on the spot, and no-one seemed to know where it was. (In Coley Park, Head Warden Nash had put out a bomb by smothering it with sand bags – buckets of sand would be kept at wardens posts and in some areas sandbags would be piled ready for use). A sandbag was found from Goldsmit Road – but burst when it was picked up. Despite this enough was left to put the Baker Street incendiary out.

Reading - New Town - Earley and Woodley

In the 1940s "Earley" covered the area roughly from Palmer Park to the boundary with Woodley around Bulmershe. Although we think of this as Reading, the administrative boundary put, for example, all of the extensive Suttons Seeds trial grounds outside the area covered by the Corporation's civil defence services.

At the time this was noted as a problem, and the two town councils petitioned both Reading and the Civil Defence Committee for Berkshire for inclusion in Reading's scheme. The residents pointed out that they lived right next to people covered by Reading's ARP services, which were at a higher level than those for Wokingham, and close to the airfield at Woodley.

On 11th September 1940, the County Council's Civil Defence Committee heard from a deputation from the Earley and Woodley Residents Shelter Association asking that their parishes be placed "on the same footing as regards air raid shelters etc, as the County Borough of Reading". The deputation included representatives from trades unions, and the meeting to hear the petition also invited representatives of the aerodrome and Ministry of Aircraft Production. As a sidenote, the residents' deputation was led by Louis Victor Smith, born in

Early Closing Day

Reading, and who, as a young officer, had commanded one of the first tanks to go into action in September 1916.[29]

Although the Ministry of Home Security said that it was not possible to cover Woodley and Earley in the same way as Reading, the County Council supported the application, and Wokingham Rural District Council agreed to build shelters within the 1000 yard radius of the aerodrome. Shelters were also built on the playing fields in Woodley and on the Sol Joel playing fields in Earley. Records in the Berkshire Record Office also mention shelters in, for example, Eastcourt Avenue and Anderson Avenue, Earley and Headley and Colemans Moor Road in Woodley.[30] An application from Woodley for its own First Aid Post was turned down. The post at St Peter's Church of England School in Earley was intended to serve both communities.[31]

The split in responsibility also has a practical impact on research today, as at the time of writing, only summary notes from outside Reading have been located, so one of the most bombed areas locally can only be documented at a very patchy level.[32] By August 1940, Woodley had shelter provision for 1344 people, in twenty eight shelters concentrating on those within 1000 yards of the Airfield.[33]

1940

16th August, 17.57. Four HE bombs dropped on Woodley. Of these, one did not explode until 05.10 the following morning. The log book of No 8 Elementary Flight Training School (EFTS) at the airfield noted that one Miles Magister trainer was damaged. [34]

12th September, 02.50 - Woodley - Eight HE and "many" incendiaries started heath fires near South Lake

12th September, 13.00 – Earley – Three bombs on Great Western Railway (GWR) line north of the Gasworks. The railway was damaged but in operation by 19.30

16th September, 15.45 – [Woodley?] – Ten HE with one unexploded (UXB) on "aerodrome" which was cleared at 08.53 on the 17th. No 8 EFTS recorded 10 bombs.

30th September – Earley – Six HE, three in Erlegh Court Gardens and three on Suttons Trial Grounds

3rd October, 15.20 – Woodley – Four HE. No8 EFTS at the airfield noted six bombs of which three were delayed action.

6th October, 09.05 – Woodley – Three HE. One person slightly injured and two houses wrecked. No 8 EFTS recorded two bombs falling on allotments north of the aerodrome

12th October, 01.48-02.20 – Earley - Four HE in and near Bulmershe Woods

1st December, 22.05 – Earley   - One "OIB" – This was an "Oil incendiary", probably a Flam 250 or 500, a standard bomb casing adapted with a liquid incendiary filling.[35]

1941

30th January, 16.15 – Woodley – two "small" HE east of Butts Hill Road.

9th/10th May – Earley – Ten HE and three incendiaries in a line across Suttons Trial Grounds 1000 yards S and E of the gasworks. One UXB

12th May, 01.45 –   Earley/Reading – A low flying aircraft machine gunned Reading Gasworks in Kings Road. Damage to one gasholder.[36]

This raid was reported by the Reading ARP services, although that on 12th May was not. The gasholder hit was "perforated in twelve places" and three minor fires were started. The gas was transferred to an adjacent holder and the damage was repaired within twelve hours.

1942

22nd June, 01.20 – Woodley – Two HE 30yds south of North Lake and 20yards East of Crockhamwell Lane 150 yards N of junction with Ford Lane. One UXB.

Writing in 2011, "Bentley" recalled the raid of June 1942 and 12th September 1940. [37]

One of the two bombs on the 22nd of June 1942 was rumoured to have fallen into the North Lake. The other landed in Richardsons field just off CROCKHAMWELL Road. It had tunnelled its way towards the road and left quite a neat hole. The Army excavated it and removed the detonator. I believe they then steamed the HE (TNT?) out. We were then allowed to view the scene. Shortly afterwards somebody pinched the detonator.

The incendiaries of the 12 Sept 1940 mostly fell in the South Lake woods, known locally as Baileys woods. Some fell nearer the railway in the wood on the left ,Kennedys woods. We found one of the incendiaries intact, took it home and got a real rollicking. PC Hunt from Loddon Bridge Rd arrived to take it away.

Early Closing Day

Another HE device made a big hole next to the railway line by the level crossing.

The bombs which fell in daylight on Woodley aerodrome must have been while I was at Woodley CofE school. We had to get under the desks for shelter but I don't know the date.

In 1999 a single SC1000 1000KG bomb was unearthed during work within 200 metres of the railway at Woodley. The casing is now in the Berkshire Museum of Aviation.[38] The incident was remembered by Noel Chappell as being in November 1941 although the details of his recollection fit the raid of 16th August, as he recalled

A stick of bombs came down through the clouds, there were four of them, definitely four, I am absolutely certain of that. There was a dull thud and big heaps of earth and clay flew into the air. This was about 400 - 500 yards away from where we were standing.
Two bombs exploded and there were two craters.[39]

The raid of October 6th 1940 may be that recalled by Lewis Budd in an interview with the Berkshire Museum of Aviation. [40] He recalled bombs were dropped in the allotments opposite the training school and the old cottages in Headley Road were blown up. Mr Budd stated that one of them belonged to Mr. Lee who had the off licence and bakery in Headley Road, these cottages were so old and decrepit that they might just have fallen down from the blast even if they did not receive a direct hit. He identified the aircraft that actually hit the airfield as a Junkers Ju88.

1944

19th **June**, 22.25 – Reading – V1 "Flying Bomb" fell near Beech Lane and Wilderness Road ("Radstock Farm") causing four slight casualties and damage to houses.

The Flying Bomb incident - one of twelve in Berkshire - is recalled by a number of eye-witnesses who remember the distinctive – and ominous - sound of the weapon's pulse-jet motor. The missile carried an 850kg (1870lb) high explosive warhead.

The Reading Civil Defence Committee noted only that an "air raid incident..." had caused "slight damage to the property known as 32 Elm Road". [41] On 23rd June the *Berkshire Chronicle* published a photograph believed to show damage caused by this V1. The photograph shows a "Mr Mathews" and a "Mrs Morse" and the text noted that the weapon destroyed a hedge and crops. [42]

Given a level speed of about 400mph, the V1 was around fourteen seconds from the town centre, but its course is not known.[43] V1 attacks began on 13th June 1944, and so this missile would have been one of the first few hundred launched from northern France by the Luftwaffe's Flak Regiment 155 (W). The bombs were fired from fixed ramps aligned on London, initially giving an average point of impact around Dulwich. In theory the V1 had a range of about 130 miles at this time so Earley was, again, in theory, well beyond the point at which it should have crashed. Whatever else can be said about this incident, Reading was almost certainly not the target.

The nearest Reading came to attack by the second "V-weapon" was on 19th March 1945 when a V2 missile exploded over Cockpole Green, near Wargrave. Its warhead fell, damaging five cottages and two pubs and causing a dozen casualties.[44]

Tilehurst
No actual raids on the part of Tilehurst that came within the Reading boundary were logged, although air raid wardens reported that a bullet from the aircraft which attacked Reading on 10th February 1943 struck a cold store at the foot of Norcot Road. [45] On 19th November 1940 an unexploded bomb was found in Westwood Farm near Westwood Row.[46]

The County incident log records one bombing related incident for Tilehurst itself, along with incidents in Tidmarsh and Purley on the Tilehurst border. [47]

5th November 1940, 19.25 – Tilehurst – 23 HE north-west of Blagrave Hospital leaving 6 UXBs – one in hospital grounds, two in Langley Hill and three between "Sulham Ridge and Sulham Lane". Damage caused in Langley Hill and Sulham

The unexploded bomb from Westwood Farm on 19th November would seem to be too far way to be associated with this raid, and the contemporary account sheds no further light on its origin.

The raids on Purley and Tidmarsh were all in winter 1940:

27th October – Purley – three unignited "flares". This entry is unclear and may refer to September 27th.

7th November, 00.10 – Tidmarsh – Four HE in Great Bear Wood

16th November, 00.01 – Pangbourne/Tidmarsh – One HE and incendiaries

Early Closing Day

19th November, 06.03 – Purley – 2 HE dropped north and west of searchlight post in Long Lane.

The internet *History of Purley on Thames* records bombs dropped between Long Lane and Sulham Woods, and confirms the existence of a searchlight post in the area. [48]

Woodley aerodrome in the late 1938.
Although at this resolution it is not possible to be completely certain, many of the he aircraft shown seem to be Miles Magisters or Hawks. Miles Aircraft factory is top left, the Air Ministry Flying School, administered by Phillips and Powis, is in the centre, and the Reading Aero Club building, later to become The Falcon public house, is bottom right.
(Image and caption Reading Libraries 1183997)

Chapter 2

Conclusion

Without knowing what the Luftwaffe was trying to achieve in its attacks on Reading covered in this chapter, it is not possible to come to any real evaluation of these raids.

At no time does any serious attempt to attack the town seem to have been made.

The main railway line was disrupted on a couple of occasions, albeit very briefly. Properties were destroyed and, if Reading followed the pattern of other towns and cities subjected to bombing, some absenteeism will have occurred possibly causing some loss to production; people working on ARP duties will have been distracted from other tasks, and simply worn out by a lack of sleep.

The raid of 7th November 1940 did place bombs accurately over a useful target, but failed to cause real problems.

Only the raid of January 1941 on Caversham seems to have tested the ARP services to any real extent, and this one raid caused more property damage than all the others combined until that of 1943 on the town centre. It marked the nearest the Germans ever came to causing widespread fires, but although hundreds of bomblets were dropped, they never achieved the concentration needed to set major fires.

It has been argued here that the attacks on Reading during 1940-41 should be regarded, like the majority of attacks on targets in Britain at the time, as purely nuisance attacks. It is, of course, very hard to quantify "nuisance", and the reality of the threat meant that Reading could not relax its guard. However, this did not mean that significant additional resources were put into ARP (even after petitions from local groups) beyond creating a demand for sleeping space in shelters.

Whilst people were injured, and homes and businesses damaged or destroyed, the scale – if not the personal impact – was minimal.

Early Closing Day

Chapter Two Notes

1. Berkshire County Council Civil Defence Committee minutes at Berkshire Records Office C/CL/C3/19/1
2. Figures from Overy, Richard. *The Bombing War*, London 2013
3. Colin Dobinson. *Fields of Deception* (2000) p. 69
4. Overy, op.cit..
5. Collier, B. *Defence of the United Kingdom*. HMSO, 1957. Appendix XVII
6. Ibid.
7. Hastings, Max. *Bomber Command*. Pan, 1981. Appendix E
8. Collier, B (1957) Chapter XVII
9. Berkshire County Control Centre siren and incident log at BRO C/D/2/1
10 From reports in BRO File D/EX 1657/2. The German SC50 50kg bomb meets   this description
11. Reading Corporation Emergency Committee minutes 28th October 1940 at BRO R/AC2/20/1A
12. Reading forum 22 May 2010. Last accessed on 7th February 2011
13. The author would like to express his thanks to Dora Nash of the Oratory School who kindly provided this information
14 DVD, London Channel 4 Television, 2010
15 http://www.hiddenlives.org.uk/homes/EMMER01.html accessed on 6/12/11
16 http://thedaysofglory2.blogspot.co.uk/2010/08/luftwaffe-bombs.html accessed on 16/10/2015
17 Hiddenlives.org.uk   Op.cit.
18. Cliffe [2007], pp.40
19. From notes from 2008 on the internet at www.getreading.co.uk/community
20. http://www.bmcole.co.uk/coloptics/luftwaffe/A4-READING.htm
21. http://www.historyofreadingsociety.org.uk/?page_id=44 last accessed on 23rd February 2016
22. BRO D/EX 1650/1.
23. John H on Reading Forum 06.02.13. The Branch Line, which closed in 1983, is described at http://www.coleypark.com/cp_rambling.htm.
24 Reading: WEA, 1977. Reference kindly provided by Ann Smith of Reading   . Library
25. BRO CD/2/2
26. Lyne Goddard, pers. comm. To the author, 09.02.12
27. Reading Forum 05.02.13 last accessed on 14.02.13.
28. BRO D/EX1942/2/2/33
29. http://www.firsttankcrews.com/tankcrewsc13toc18.htm last accessed 31/12/2015
30.   Berkshire Records Office. Records of Civil Defence and Emergency Planning,   . Berkshire County Council. Undated finding guide.
31. Ibid.
32. BRO CD/2/1-3

33. Berkshire County Council Civil Defence Committee minutes for 28th August 1940, in BRO C/CL/C3/19/1

34.   Notes taken from display in Berkshire Museum of Aviation, 13.09.12

35.   SEE Note viii

36.   BRO D/EX/1657/237

37.   Reading Forum 01/11/2011 Last accessed on 7th February 2011

38.   http://news.bbc.co.uk/1/hi/uk/480871.stm last accessed on 7th February 2011 and http://home.comcast.net/~aero51/html/exhibits/bomb.htm

39.   Ibid.

40.   Ibid

41.   Meeting of 30th June 1944.

42.   The photograph and notes from Reading Museum are online at http://collections.readingmuseum.org.uk/index.asp?page=record&mwsquery={totopic}={Reading and the Second World War}& filename=REDMG&hitsStart=97 last accessed on 22nd February 2016

43.   The general information on the V1 in this section is taken from Norman Longmate. *The Doodlebugs*. Hutchinson, 1981 and Collier (See bibliography)

44.   BRO CD/2//3

45.   BRO D/EX/1657/2

46.   ibid

47.   BRO CD/2/2

48.   http://project-purley.eu/N1290.htm last accessed on 27/2/12

Early Closing Day

Dornier Do217E in flight.
This is not an aircraft of KG40 – it's from a reconnaissance unit (NAG 5) operating over Russia – but the image captures the distinctive appearance of the bomber well.
(Tom Laemlein, Armor Plate Press)

Chapter 3
The People's Pantry, 10th February 1943

The British and Americans were destroying German cities one after another ...
We...had to do the best we could with the limited resources available.

Oberst Dietrich Pelt, Angriffsfurher England from March 1943,
(Speaking post war.)[1]

The Germans

Although it is not possible to be certain, it seems probable that the fatal air raid on Reading on 10th February 1943 was carried out by a Dornier Do217E-4 of the unit 5/II/KG40 – 5th Staffel (Squadron) 2nd Gruppe, Kampgeschwader 40.[2]

Eyewitnesses at the time, including Civil Defence personnel and individuals trained in aircraft recognition, identified the bomber as a Dornier Do217. The Do217 was the only German bomber operational in the west with twin tail fins, a clear recognition feature.

The aircraft that bombed Newbury at 16.35 that afternoon, and which, it is believed, was shot down at about 16.50 over Tangmere airfield, was identified as being from 5/II/KG40 as was the only other Do217 shot down that day, at about 16.30 over Saltdean.[3] (Witnessed by a Reading fireman who was on a training course).[4] The Tangmere Dornier certainly carried the F8 unit code of KG40.[5]

5/II/KG40 was operating under the command of KG2 at this time, and KG2's own records show the unit to have been operational over Britain on the afternoon of 10th February.[6] KG2 itself came under the command of Luftflotte 3, which covered operations based in Holland, Belgium and France.[7] Luftflotte 3 could deploy just over 100 serviceable bombers, and around the same number of fighter bombers at around the time of the raid on Reading. (To set this in proportion, RAF Bomber Command *lost* just over 100 aircraft on night operations in February 1943 alone).[8]

Anything more precise than this is not possible at the time of writing. It is possible that the Reading bomber came from another unit within KG2, but there are such close parallels between the attack on Newbury and that on Reading that it is hard to believe that the two crews were not operating together and possibly briefed together.

Without access to KG40 records, which have been stated to have been lost, [9] it

Early Closing Day

is also not possible to state exactly what the German crew were seeking to bomb, and local speculation can only remain just that. In the author's opinion it is highly unlikely that any single building in Reading was the target, or, indeed, was capable of being hit, by that crew on that day.

The general mission for bomber units in the West had been set by Hitler in April the previous year -

When targets are selected, preference is to be given to those where attacks are likely to have the greatest effect on civilian life ... terror attacks of a retaliatory nature are to be carried out on towns other than London. [10]

The German air attacks of 1940 and 1941 had had specific objectives: destroy RAF Fighter Command and then bomb Britain into submission. From 1942, German bombing strategy over Britain was as vague or as precise as any interpretation possible for Hitler's statement.

What was known as the "Baedeker Blitz", after the popular tourist guides from which both sides thought targets were selected, started in April 1942, and whilst it had petered out by the winter of 1942-43, bombing continued. Tactics changed during the period, with the initial night attacks by between 10-30 planes on a given target giving way to low level daytime attacks by single aircraft such as those on 10th February 1943.

With a bomber strength in the West of just over one hundred serviceable aircraft – most of the Luftwaffe's bomber force was either in Russia or in the Mediterranean – this was the effective limit of German capability.

In the background to this, targets within range of fighter bombers – chiefly towns along the South Coast – were subject to fast "hit and run" raids, which proved hard to counter.

Night bombing continued during 1943, but resumed more aggressively in January-May 1944, in a campaign known to the Luftwaffe as Operation Steinbock and to the British as the "Baby Blitz". Raids of, typically, 100-200 aircraft hit London repeatedly, but also ranged as far as Hull and Falmouth. The aim of these attacks was retaliation for RAF attacks on Germany cities – as it had been in 1942-43 – but with the intention that the attacks would be of such a scale that the Allies would not risk further severe raids of their own.[11]

As such, the offensive failed, and attacks on Britain passed to the "V-Weapons", such as the V1 Flying Bomb which fell on Earley in June 1944, as noted in Chapter 2.

Chapter 3

When 5/II/KG40 was formed it was equipped with the Do217, and was ultimately to move over to KG2 permanently. The unit had twenty nine Do217E -4s on strength at February 1943. The Dornier 217E4 was the main operational type of the family, powered by two BMW radial engines, and capable of up to 320 mph with a range of about 1300 miles. Although the attack on 10th February was made down at 150ft, the Do217 had an operation ceiling of 24-25,000ft. [12] Just over 1900 were built.

The Dornier that bombed Reading carried four 1100lb SC500 bombs, around its maximum load. As noted in Chapter 2, this meant that it was lifting half to a third of the bomb load of a contemporary British heavy bomber, for example the Avro Lancaster, and about the same as a light or medium bomber such as the DeHavilland Mosquito or Douglas Boston, both in RAF service at this time.

In addition to its bombload, the Do217E-4, a version modified for attacks on shipping, carried up to six machine guns: three 7.92mm guns in the nose and cockpit sides, a fixed 15mm gun in the nose and two 13mm machine guns, one in a turret at the upper rear of the cockpit, the other in the lower rear end of the cockpit. [13]

At the time of the raid on Reading, II Gruppe was commanded by Major Martin Kästner. 5th Staffel's commander, Oberleutnant Hans Kleeman, was killed when his Dornier was shot down by anti aircraft over Tangmere on the afternoon of 10th February. Kleeman and his crew are buried in Tangmere and in Chichester. [14]

The Gruppe was based at Soesterberg, a former Dutch air force base near Utrecht, but this does not necessarily mean that 5th Staffel was flying from there in February 1943.

If it was, the straight line distance from Soesterberg to Reading would have taken the crew just over an hour at full speed, but it is highly likely that they would have taken a course down the North Sea to cross the English coast somewhere in Sussex: One aircraft of the unit was shot down over Saltdean and Luftwaffe aerial photographs gave Beachy Head and Selsey Bill as navigational way points to Reading.[15] Navigation would have been done by map reading at speed at low level, and by "dead reckoning" – timed runs from known points. Full speed all the way would have gobbled fuel, so may only have been used on the run in. German records show that the take off time for the missions flown that afternoon was between approximately 3pm and 4pm.[16]

KG2 and KG40 sent twenty nine aircraft to attack UK targets. Thirteen did not

Early Closing Day

bomb due to cloud cover over, with the remainder reporting that they had bombed between 4.20pm and 6.10pm. The times reported suggest two phases – attacks from 4.20 until around 4.45, and then from 5.40 until 6.10. The targets hit at around the same time as Reading were -

Brighton   Chichester   Horsham

Hosham   Newbury   Tangmere

"Petwrith"   Worthing (twice).

"Petwrith" may refer to Petworth in West Sussex, but this is unconfirmed.

Without German records it is impossible to reconstruct their side of the raid on Reading that day accurately, but some general background can help set the scene.

A diagram of the attack run used on Cardiff in Spring 1943 shows tactics used by KG2 at the time. The aircraft approached across the English Channel at a height of around 150-400 feet to keep them "below" the reach of the British Chain Home Ultra Low Radar, that was just coming into use, until as close to the coast as possible. Detection meant interception was more likely, and any attack would be made across territory, at the very least, defended by alert anti-aircraft gunners if not fighters. As noted above, two Dornier crews that afternoon were killed by these defences.

Assuming that they followed standard practice, in the air the crew that bombed Reading would have been commanded by the navigator – "observer" (Beobachter) in Luftwaffe terminology - regardless of rank, unlike RAF practice where the pilot led. [17]

Civil Defence in Reading town centre. [18]
As discussed in Chapter 2, preparation for any air attack on Reading had begun with the centre of the town.

By 1943 the public shelter programme was effectively complete, giving spaces for well over 2000 people in basements under the shops of Broad Street, Friar Street and the streets in between. Just as an example, Queen Victoria Street offered shelter spaces for 300.

The largest shelters were under the ARP Offices and Miss Reid's shop in Market Place – 405 places – and under Wellsteeds in Broad Street, with room for 443.

The closest air raid siren to the town centre was on the Town Hall itself, with the main Report and Control Centre in its basement.

Given the lack of homes in the shopping centre, only one Warden's Post covered the main area – post D5 in Market Passage.

There was a First Aid Post in Silver Street – although Simond's Brewery on Bridge Street also had first aid facilities - and the closest First Aid Party depot was on Castle Hill, with the nearest rescue party in Abattoirs Road.

The closest fire engines were at the part time location in Friar Street, in St Mary's Butts and Caversham Road Station.

Central Reading, February 10th 1943

Including individual incendiaries, something over 400 bombs fell on the Reading area during the Second World War.

Only four of these fell on the centre of the town, but these four caused more casualties that all the others combined and it is this one event that has most penetrated the community's memory.

Some aspects of this raid, delivered at tea time on a Wednesday, are firmly established in the historical record - detailed reports survive from Reading's civil defence services, for example. Other features are perhaps unrecoverable – the names of all those injured, and the exact German intentions. Alongside this a wide range of oral history and local memory has added personal, human colour, but sometimes at the expense of accuracy.   That is not to say that these accounts are in some way "wrong", but that they cannot always be cross checked against other information.   This account will concentrate on information from primary sources.

The bombing will be dealt with as two separate incidents, following the breakdown used by Reading's ARP services in their handling and reporting in 1943 -

Incident 1 - Minster St/Wellsteeds   Incident 2 - People's Pantry/Town Hall

Early Closing Day

Wednesday 10th February 1943 was early closing day.

At about half past four spotters on top of H.G Simond's Brewery saw a single Dornier Do217 bomber approaching fast and low from the direction of Burghfield (the south east). They sounded the works alarm.

This was timed as 16.29 in a later incident report, and at 16.32 by the Head

Early Closing Day

Warden of A Group in his report written on the day. The County Siren Log notes the Red Alert as happening at 16.30.[19]

The Ministry of Works Chief Scientific Advisor noted later that the alarm had no effect beyond the ARP services - *Hitherto no bombs have fallen in Reading. The Air Raid Warning seems to have been ignored entirely by the inhabitants.* [20]

Since Woodley was bombed the previous May, there had been sixteen Red Alerts in Reading Warning Area, but no attacks. Given only five to six minutes warning it is hard to see that many of the casualties could have been avoided if people had responded to the sirens and the town centre shelters had been used.

The Simond's spotters noted the Dornier at 150ft.   The incident report in the National Archives gives the aircraft as being spotted by the Royal Observer Corps at 500ft, with an eyewitness from the RAF, Flying Officer Caltin, quoted as giving its height as 150ft.[21] The German records said the attack was from 50 metres.[22]

Although apparently a detail, it may be that the aircraft's height played a critical factor in determining the results of the raid.

As discussed above, the Do217 was most probably from the Luftwaffe's 5th Staffel II/KG40, and was attacking Reading simultaneously with an attack on Newbury.[23]

At about 16.34 – contemporary accounts give it as 16.34 to 16.36 - the Dornier released four SC500 1100lb bombs and, according to eyewitnesses at the time, opened fire with its machine guns.

The Head Warden of D Group, returning from a trip to London, reported the sound of falling bombs and machine-gunning at the same time as he emerged from the subway at Reading Station.[24] One account, from Inspector Seager of the police, stated that the aircraft opened fire before the explosion of bombs was heard.

The most common reaction to the incident today is puzzlement at why the Luftwaffe should bother to bomb Reading, and speculation as to the target.

At the time, in a lecture to ARP wardens Mr L. J. Pollard of the Rescue Service concluded that, allowing for course and estimated speed, the most probable point of aim was the Southern Railways Station. Pollard argued that the German bomb-aimer had been misled by his altimeter into thinking that he was at 200ft

Chapter 3

rather than 150, and, ironically, had bombed accurately on the basis of that assumption. The result was that instead of hitting the railway he hit the town.[25] A surviving Luftwaffe target map of Reading gives some credence to this view – the map shows the station and bridge over the Thames in the direct path of the bombs dropped.[26] The KG2 War Diary simply states that the town centre was bombed.

The four SC500s fell as follows

Bomb 1 – Next to Fuller's paint store in Earley Place, south of Minster Street

Bomb 2 – Passed through Reading Labour Hall in Minster Street, exploding in Wellsteeds department store

Bomb 3 – Passed through the upper storeys of a shop, bursting in a yard outside the People's Pantry restaurant

Bomb 4 – Passed through the attic of the People's Pantry, destroying a BBC "H" radio transmitter before detonating on the pavement 9ft from the Town Hall's southern tower.

The Minster St Incident – Bombs 1 and 2

In order for them to have landed where they did, the Dornier would have had to have released its bombs about 270 metres – around 300 yards - before the first impact – somewhere approximately over Southampton St. The spread of the "stick" across Reading town centre suggests that a fraction of a second separated two pairs of bombs.

A number of eyewitnesses have described seeing the bomber on its run in, its bomb doors open and bombs falling.

Peggy Stanlake – then Peggy Clarke - for example, was at home in St John's Road, ready to go out. She was 17 at the time, and recalled what she saw when interviewed in 2015 -

> *I was standing combing my hair, ready to go out ... There were no sirens but I saw a small plane and knew it was German by the drone of the engine. As I watched I realised it wasn't 'one of ours'! ... I had been attending aircraft recognition classes with the A.R.P. (and) I had been called up to be a warden. As I watched I saw the three bombs drop. (Strangely they sort of joggled around – I'd thought that bombs went head first but these didn't.)* [27]

Early Closing Day

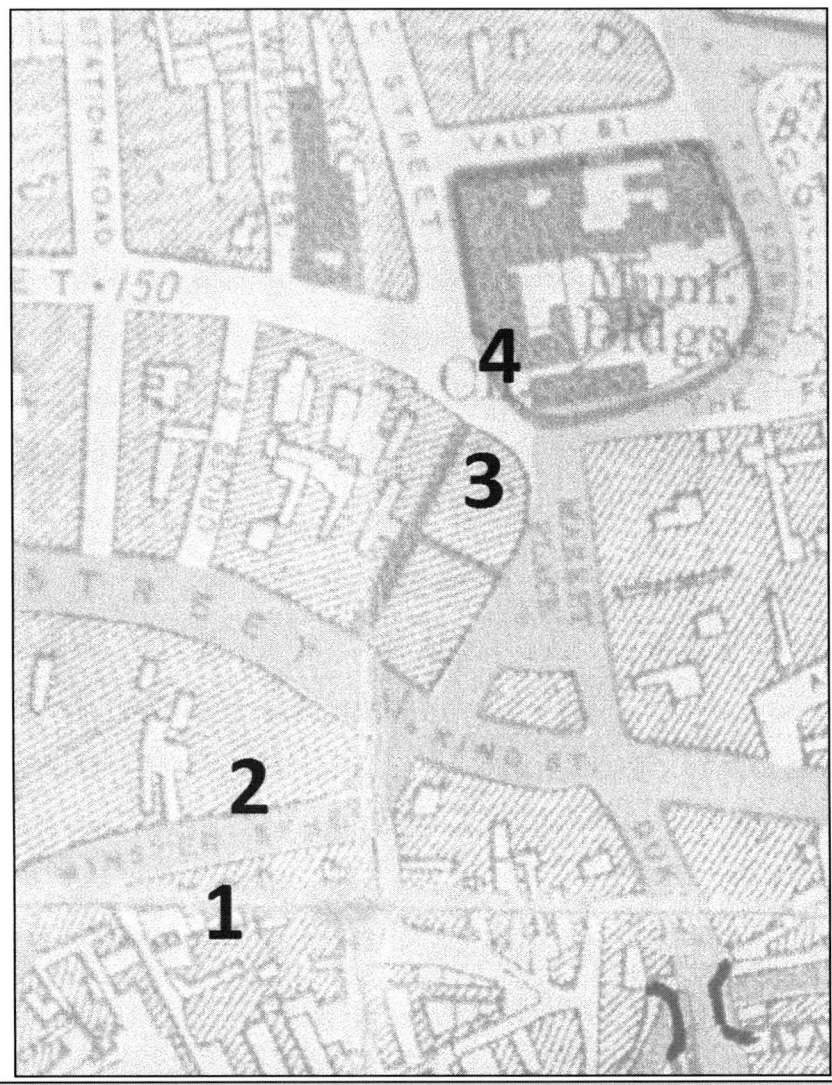

Section of a German Luftwaffe target intelligence map of Reading town centre showing the location of the four bombs which fell on 10th February 1943. Note that they form two pairs. It is based on the 1938 British Ordnance Survey.
(Reading Libraries. Photograph by Richard Marks)

Bomb 1

The first bomb to fall was timed at 16.34 in the report in the National Archives.[28]

Having hit Simond's' Brewery, it passed through a shed before detonating "within a foot or so of reinforced concrete paint store". The bomb left a twenty five foot crater, which filled with linseed oil from the store, starting a small fire.

An "armament identification form" completed on the 15th April 1943 stated that this bomb had been painted dark green, with yellow stripe on the tail. The latter was the standard Luftwaffe coding for a high explosive bomb.

No casualties were caused, but the second bomb in this incident caused three fatalities, trapped at least four people and injured "several".

Bomb 2

In 1943, the south side of Minster Street was dominated by the headquarters of Reading Trades Council and the local Labour Party at number 56 with the Reading Trades Union Club and Institute at 57-59.[29]

The Trades Union Club had a restaurant on the ground floor, with a dance hall and meeting rooms above. Early in the war the National Union of Tobacco Workers relocated to the building from London. [30]

On the north side were Watson's and Sons, glass dealers, at 13-15, the rear of Wellsteeds department store, a tailors shop, hardware shop, wine merchants and Heelas removals.

The Dornier's second bomb passed through the Reading Trades Union Club, losing its fins in the process and, incidentally, destroying the Labour Party records. It trapped Percy Belcher, the General Secretary of the Tobacco Workers Union – later taken to Royal Berkshire Hospital - and left a hole 9ft by 4ft, having bounced off a wall. Crossing Minster Street it hit the rear of Wellsteeds department store about 25ft above the pavement.

Wellsteeds had been built in the 1870s, with part of its basement reinforced in wartime to act as one of the main public shelters in the town centre. The town's Rescue Service estimated that the SC500 had been fitted with a five second delay fuse, and the bomb burst twenty five feet off the ground inside the rear of the building on the restaurant floor, demolishing it and partially

Early Closing Day

demolishing the front, Broad Street, section. Shrapnel left a hole "as big as a man's fist" in an iron girder.

Surrounding buildings in Minster Street were affected by the blast.

In a lecture to Air Raid Wardens on 21st February Mr Pollard of the Rescue Service, stated that "about half" the store had been demolished.[31] When he took his audience on a tour of the damage, grey paint "from the bomb" could be seen on the remains of one of the walls of the building – fragments found after the raid showed it to be a "dirty sand" colour with yellow stripes on the tail.

Early closing that day almost certainly saved Reading many lives. The Air Raid Damage report noted that casualties "would have been enormous". Wellsteeds' manager was quoted by the Ministry of Home Security report on the bombing as saying that, on a normal day, 120 staff and up to 150 customers would have been in the building, with at least 100 in the area actually demolished.

The manager, Augustus Haylock, would normally have been working through an early closing day, but, speaking to the *Reading Chronicle* in 2013, his grandson recalled that he had a cold that day, so had gone home early. The bomb demolished his office. [32]

Five fire watchers were inside Wellsteeds when Bomb 2 exploded. Three were injured - Miss Shirley, Miss Cope and a Miss Hutchings. All were taken to Battle Hospital, and Pollard's lecture, referred to above, stated that one, unidentified, had been seriously injured.

Outside, two girls seeking shelter in the alley between Watson's and Wellsteeds were buried in rubble and killed. Betty Parsons was 11 and Violet Brown, 10. With them was Clarence Brown, Violet Brown's brother. He was rescued suffering from shock and taken to the Royal Berkshire Hospital.

Another fatality occurred in a yard "at the back of the Cheddar Cheese Pub" - James Doran lived at 3 Greyfriars Road and was 62.

Ivy Kowalkawski, then Ivy Parsons, was with Betty, her sister, and her friend Violet Brown. Writing in a letter to the *Evening Post* in 1999 she remembered

We were coming from St. Mary's School in Hosier Street, walking down Minster

Bomb damage in Fuller's yard, 11th February 1943.
The first bomb to fall on the 10th February went off next to a paint store in Earley Place.
The photograph and plan here are part of a set prepared for the incident report.
(Reading Libraries 9158)

Street when I looked up and saw a German plane and there was such   a bang.
Everything went black and I shouted "Run girls". It was all so quiet   and scary
with dust and debris flying everywhere...I was covered in blood   from head to
toe.[33]

Mrs Kowalkawski spent the next three weeks in hospital, so was clearly lucky to have survived.

Blast and debris from the bomb hit buildings on the south side of Broad St from "Hayes Outfitters" next to Hughes Wholesale Tobacconists. Three people in Hughes were injured, one in the Heelas Depository to the rear of Wellsteeds, and the first aid post at Simond's Brewery treated several cases. [34]

Early Closing Day

Bomb 3 - The People's Pantry

The third bomb dropped caused the most casualties.

Minster Street, 11th February 1943.
Looking towards Gun Street, showing the Trades Union Club and Labour Party offices on the left. The second bomb caused the damage visible before exploding in Wellsteeds on the right hand side of the road.
(Reading Libraries)

The People's Pantry occupied the first floor, ground floor and the basement of 175 Friar St, a three storey Victorian building converted for the purpose.[35] On the top floor was a BBC "H" Transmitting station.[36]

The restaurant had a staff of thirty seven. Part of a chain of over 1990 "British Restaurants" across the country – 114 of which were in the South East - it was intended to offer people the chance to buy a cheap, nutritious midday meal to supplement their rations.

Watson and Son, china and glass dealers, Minister Street, 18th February 1943.
This is on the north side of the street, backing onto Broad Street. The damage to A.R.Saunders next door and to Wellsteeds is very clear to the right of Watson's.
(Reading Libraries 1392036).

The idea drew on experience with state-supported works canteens. By February 1943 British Restaurants were serving over 540,000 midday meals a day.[37] In the South East the total was just under 16,800 meals a day.[38] Most were run by local authorities, with a small number solely by the voluntary sector.

The People's Pantry would have joined Emergency Feeding Centres and mobile canteens in distributing pre-cooked meals to people made homeless or left without cooking facilities in the event of a serious raid. As mentioned in Chapter 1, the aim of the Feeding Centres was to give 10% of the population 12 meals over three or four days.

Early Closing Day

Wellsteed's restaurant in about 1935.
The restaurant was a feature of the refitted store.
(Reading Libraries 1392024)

The restaurant was run by the Corporation with support from the Ministry of Food, and was staffed by Women's Voluntary Service (WVS) volunteers. The Air Raid Damage Report on the bombing stated that the People's Pantry had a staff of 37 and could seat 100 people with tables seating six each.

An unnamed "official" quoted in the *Gloucester Citizen* on the 11th February stated that *the restaurant would normally have been well filled. It seated more than two hundred.* [39]

The nature of newspaper reporting of this raid is discussed, briefly, below in the 'Conclusion', but this was fairly clearly a syndicated article or one originating with a Ministry of Information briefing.

In 1941, apparently lobbying for a British Restaurant in its own town, after a letter from Lord Woolton (Minister of Food) urging more progress, the *Portsmouth Evening News* gave a description of the then new People's Pantry.[40] (Portsmouth had been raided the night before by just over 150 aircraft, dropping 148 tons of high explosive bombs and over 1400 incendiary clusters [41]).

Pantries for the People

...What can be done in one case can be done in all...

That communal kitchens are meeting a real need may be inferred from the Reading communal feeding centre. It is called The People's Pantry and is open seven days a week from 8am to 9pm. Right from the start [no date is given] the People's Pantry was a success providing between 600 and 900 dinners daily and being patronised each day by about 8000 persons.

It may be noted that the Ministry of Food had arranged for stocks of provisions to be available for feeding centres as well as financial help for up to one hundred per cent grant for capital outlay.

All the authorities have to do is lay in supplies of fuel and enlist necessary helpers

If the Portsmouth newspaper's figures are correct, the People's Pantry was already well used possibly only a month after it opened. It was well placed in the town centre, and in a position to do just what it was designed to do, act as a

Inside Wellsteeds' Restaurant .18th February 1943.
Shown a week after the 1100lb bomb that struck the building on 10th February exploded in this area. According to a 1920s booklet published by Wellsteeds *Shopping in Reading*, the restaurant had a capacity of 274 and a "permanent orchestra".
(Roger Peacock Collection/Reading Libraries 1392025)

Early Closing Day

surrogate works canteen for office and shop workers to allow them to stretch their ration by buying a cheap, but solid and nourishing, midday meal.

An advertisement in the *Berkshire Chronicle* in 1940 said that the People's Pantry offered *Something to eat for 2d All you can eat for 6d.* [42]

In his autobiography *Six spoons of sugar*, published in 2008, Richard Holdsworth, who was an evacuee living in Upper Basildon, recalls hearing that People's Pantry offered "A square meal at a fair price". [43]

The building had been a wallpaper store, owned by John Botterill, and the advert, quoted above, also showed that it had been taken over with support from Simond's Brewery.

Alongside, in 172-174 were offices and the Victorian Arcade linking Friar Street to Broad Street, home to over a dozen small shops and businesses.

As with the second bomb, the third did not detonate on its first impact and may reasonably be assumed to have had the same delay fusing as the second. The aim would have been to allow the bomb to penetrate a building before exploding, or to cause a larger crater in the ground.

Hitting the wooden rear extension to a shop, the sandy coloured SC500 passed through the top storey of the building next door to the People's Pantry before clipping the corner of the first floor of the restaurant.[35] The 220 kilos of explosive filling burst either in the restaurant yard, or just next door, about 6-8ft up. Although the post raid report noted that it caused only a "slight depression" the bomb caused damage over a radius of 34-72ft from its point of detonation.

The explosion demolished a 64 foot long run of wall in the Arcade next to the Pantry, and brought down two bays of the restaurant's roof, causing a third to "hinge" into the kitchen. Mr Pollard of the Rescue Service was more graphic than the official account: the bomb *carried part of the first floor and ground floor into the basement.*

In effect this dropped the restaurant into its own basement, and dropped its roof on top of it.

The Raid Summary, held in the Public Record Office contains chillingly exact details.

The majority of those killed or injured were victims of *Falling debris and...flying missiles such as the bricks of the wall near the bomb.*[46]

Chapter 3

The Arcade, Friar Street in 1902.
Number 175, which became the People's Pantry is at the left. Although left standing –
just – after the raid on 10th February. This frontage had to be demolished
(Reading Libraries 1285587)

Ten bodies were found in the yard outside the restaurant, with *Four headless corpses in the restaurant in line with the detonation of the bomb*. One victim was blown into the corner of a shop in the arcade, another into the *Transfer station at the back of Odd Fellows Hall*.

Dorothy Pateman, a WVS volunteer originally from Yorkshire, was killed in the People's Pantry as was Ellen Thompson from Whitley, who was serving customers. Two members of staff off duty were killed in the Arcade, including Catherine Byland, who was 47 and lived on Oxford Road not far from Tilehurst Station. Nine staff in the basement were injured with five of the six staff in kitchen injured, one losing her right arm.[47] The "hingeing" ceiling seems to have protected the manageress from harm.

At about a quarter past four, Edith Osbourne and Emily Parker left Southampton Street to go for tea in the People's Pantry. Both were killed there, their bodies identified the following day in mortuaries at the Co-op Works and Sackville Street.

Mrs Letch was on her way to the Palace Theatre with her husband, and had

Early Closing Day

popped into the People's Pantry for a cup of tea. Her husband knew Ellen Thompson who served them that afternoon. Mrs Letch recalled what happened in 1999. The explosion came *As soon as he left the counter...All of us sitting fell into the cellar. I could not find my husband for a while as we were all covered in debris...People lay there injured and were screaming.*[48]

The Town Hall, Blandy's, St Laurence's and the Arcade in about 1893. 175 Friar St is just visible next to the Arcade at the Left. Although taken 50 years earlier. The area had changed very little in general appearance by 1943. (Reading Libraries 1236413)

In the Arcade, Warden Shrosbree was trapped by the bomb, but on extricating himself remembered that he had just passed three women and three boys, whom he rescued single handedly.

Sixty one year old William Hooban, a Post Office worker was less fortunate. His family remembered that had gone into the People's Pantry for a cup of tea at the end of his shift, and was killed in the Arcade.[49]

Just round the corner in Market Place – virtually next door - the bomb damaged the headquarters of Wardens Group D in Market Passage and "partially wrecked" the WVS Office in the same location. Senior Warden Cross was commended for making it to the Report Centre with his report even though affected by the bomb.

Again, Senior Warden Cross was perhaps lucky - three people were killed in Market Place and Market Street with four more in 29 Market Place, which was a cluster of small businesses around Arthur Cooper's Wine Merchants. The dead included PC Rex Jupp, from Ennerdale Road in Whitley, and Edward Eaton, a warden from Southampton.

As was often the case that afternoon, timing prevented the incident from being much worse. The WVS was running a Basic Training class for fifty members in its headquarters in Market Passage, and Reading Centre's report for the month recorded the *narrow escape of [the class] when the room in which the talk was given was demolished within five minutes of the class dispersing.* [50]

Bomb 4

The fourth bomb also struck the People's Pantry, passing straight through its upper floor to burst outside the Town Hall.

On its way through 175 Friar Street the bomb demolished the BBC "H" transmitter in the attic, injuring two of the four personnel. [51]

The bomb detonated 9ft from the Town Hall tower, leaving a crater 18ft in diameter and three foot deep, and collapsing the frontage of Blandy's solicitors into the crater, also causing structural damage to the front of St Laurence's Church.

In the Town Hall itself, the ceiling of the Mayor's Parlour was brought down and windows blown in. A low wall of cement blocks was blown into a basement passage, fatally injuring a woman worker, Margaret Thackeray, who was from Emmer Green, and damaging the main Reporting Centre.

Blast from the bomb also damaged the front of the People's Pantry, and the Raid Summary pointed out that it was not possible to be certain which casualties were caused by this bomb as opposed to the third.

Derek Chamberlain was just outside the People's Pantry when the third and fourth bombs fell.

He was 14 at the time, and had been moved from Whitstable in Kent to Reading

Early Closing Day

by his father at the outbreak of war. He went to Battle School, and lived with his brother and two sisters in his grandmother's house in Prince of Wales Avenue.[52]

In 2012 he was interviewed by Reading Museum, and what follows is taken from this account.

Derek went to school as usual on what he recalled was a damp dismal day. He'd arranged to meet his friend, John Nolan, outside the Arcade in Friar Street at 4.30. He hoped John would have some cigarettes with him.

He went into the People's Pantry and had a cup of tea to warm himself up. Inside were 40-60 people. It was crowded, but cheap and the chairs were comfortable. Finishing his tea, he climbed the steps back to Friar St and checked the Town Hall clock: it was 4.34.

Derek didn't see the Dornier, but he heard and saw the bomb falling. The sirens went shortly before the bombs hit, but he recalled that people disregarded them and he knew there were people still sitting drinking their tea when the bombs hit.

There was a "whoosh".

He was still facing the Town Hall. The bomb fell to the front or slightly to the side of him, and he was blown back into the Arcade and People's Pantry.

Just across the road in Blandy and Blandy's Solicitors, Frank Seymour, who lived in Hamilton Road, was killed and the owner, Ted Blandy, injured as the bomb destroyed most of the building's frontage.[53] Interviewed by the *Evening Post* in 1969, Ted Blandy recalled *[Frank Seymour had come in to] consult me on some point when the siren went. We both flung ourselves on the floor. Then the ceiling caved in and I passed out.* [54]

The Machine Gun attack

One feature of the attack which is vividly remembered, and which provokes most comment amongst modern audiences, is the machine gunning of Reading.

It's tempting to describe this as the last phase of the attack, but those there at the time did not separate the bombing and machine gunning.

As noted above, on the 19th February Inspector Seager wrote to the Chief Warden saying that on the day of the attack he was at the corner of Blagrave and Valpy Streets when a *Low enemy plane...opened fire with its guns...gunfire* *was <u>followed</u>* [author's emphasis] *by exploding bombs.*[55]

People's Pantry interior, 1940.
One of only a few photographs of the People' Pantry, this is believed to show the
basement of the restaurant at about the time of its opening in 1940.
(Reading Libraries)

Brian Kite, who was working on the Basingstoke Road, had a clear view of the Dornier from the top floor of his workplace. He taught aircraft recognition at the time, and, writing in 2012, recalled   - *Around 4.30 I noticed a Dornier 217E approach Reading on a course that took it close to Coley Park, then across Elgar Road and near St Giles Church ... I saw the turret gunner rotate his guns and fire them. Shortly afterwards I heard the sound of the bombs...* [56]

The bullets struck in an area from Market Place out to a cold storage depot at the foot of Norcot Road in Tilehurst and up into Hemdean, Albert and Blenheim Roads in Caversham. Numbers 61-63 and 67 Albert Road were hit, and in 149 Hemdean Road, a Mrs. Meadowcroft was injured – the only recorded casualty of machine gunning. Some gauge of the intensity of the machine gun fire can be gained from the log book of the then Caversham council Junior & Infant school in Hemdean Road. [57]

Early Closing Day

The People's Pantry, probably on February 11th 1943.
According to the sketch alongside, the photograph is taken looking into the building from the Friar Street side. (Reading Libraries)

11.2.1943 - During an air raid on the town yesterday afternoon an enemy plane machine gunned this school – the following damage being caused:-

Inside school

Hall – bullet hole in ceiling.

Room 4 – damaged brickwork.

Room 2 – damaged brickwork, 10 bullet holes in top windows, window sill and bottom window and frame damaged. Radiator broken, 2 bullet holes in ceiling, numerous bullet holes in black out.

Boys Lav: overhead window broken.

Inf. Corridor – small hole in window.

Outside School

2 holes in bricks in Junior wing.

2 small holes in playground.

5 holes in roof of hall – and broken coping.

Broken window of loft over hall.

Broken roof in Junior wing.

Broken tile on meal hall roof.

Damage to pillar at entry.

Caretaker's House – holes in roof. Damage to plaster in 2 bedrooms, Bullet hole in window. All teachers and children were out of the building and no-one was hurt.

Near the main focus of the bombing attack, an office worker witnessed the machine gun fire, and recalled what happened years later talking to a relative:

At this time Vivien Green (later Vivien Stark) was employed as a typist by the Midlands Employers Mutual Insurance Company, whose offices were located on Market Place. Although Vivien had heard the air raid warning siren, thinking it to be yet another false alarm, she was stood at the window looking out when the German plane approached.

Vivien recalls, "I remember seeing the pilot's face quite distinctly encased in flying helmet and goggles as he lined his aircraft up to strafe. It seemed that the pilot fired directly at me and a series of bullets struck the building in line just below the window sill." The event was over in a very few seconds but Vivien felt that time had stood still.

The building swayed with the impact of the bombs. Turning for the door Vivien believed the building to be on fire but what she took to be smoke was clouds of dust shaken free by the explosions. By good fortune Vivien escaped unharmed. [58]

During talks, given in the run up to the raid's seventieth anniversary, the author spoke to a number of eyewitnesses who recalled seeing, and in some cases avoiding, machine gun fire in Katesgrove, Stone St, off Oxford Road and Grovelands Road.

Shocking though it may be to a modern audience, it seems to have been a matter of routine for German crews to machine gun bombing targets at this time – the bomber which attacked Newbury also machine gunned the area.[59] In 1944-45 the fighters escorting Allied bombers would also strafe targets in this way.

Early Closing Day

Reading Museum holds a 13mm bullet stamped with a German manufacturers details and a 1942 date. It is recorded to have come from Caversham, and it's hard to see how the thumb sized round – which has clearly been fired as the tracer component in the base which burned brightly to allow it to be tracked has burnt out – can be other than from one of the Dornier's two 13mm MG131 machine guns. These two guns could each have fired up to around 900 such bullets a minute.

According to the Regional Situation Report on the People's Pantry bombing, after the last rounds of its machine-gun attack, the Dornier left Reading heading south west. Very much that afternoon is the subject of confusion, and as the report has the bomber approaching from "Vurfield" to the "South East" it is not impossible that someone unfamiliar with the area transposed directions.

Town Hall, Blandy's and St Laurence's church c. 1910.
A closer view showing the elaborate frontage of Blandy and Blandy's (centre) at 1 Friar Street. (Reading Libraries 1212041)

Blast damage to the Town Hall, Blandy's and St Laurence's Church.

Mela Fuller was a schoolgirl at George Palmer School on Northumberland Avenue, Whitley– now the Palmer Academy. Writing in 2016 she remembered *running home from school with frantic mothers running to meet us. I saw a German plane leaving over the Basingstoke Rd.* [60]

Either the bomber radioed in a report to its base, or it returned home, as the parent unit that day, KG2 noted in its War Diary – a daily record of events - that Reading had been bombed at 16.33 from a height of 50 metres. As mentioned above, no British fighters claimed to have shot down Do217s on 10th February

1943, and unless the Reading plane was that shot down over Tangmere, which seems to conflict with strong evidence from Newbury, the crew almost certainly got home.

At least one newspaper report on the 11th refers to three raiders being shot down. However, the third was identified as a fighter bomber, and so cannot have been the aircraft that bombed Reading – RAF Fighter Command's War Diary records a Messerschmitt Bf109 shot down over the English Channel.[61]

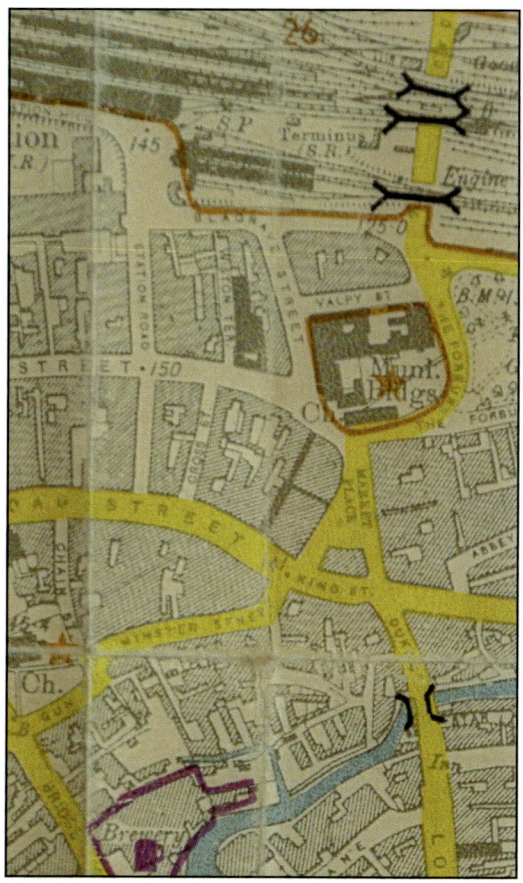

Section of a German Luftwaffe target intelligence map of Reading town centre. It is based on the 1938 British Ordnance Survey. The two railway stations show up clearly at the top of the map, with the railway and Reading Bridge clearly marked. Note that with the exception of Simond's brewery and the Town Hall no other targets are shown. (Reading Libraries. Photograph by Richard Marks)

Early Closing Day

Conclusion

The People's Pantry raid is unique amongst the set of raids on Reading during the war in that the fatalities caused meant that it was reported and studied in far greater depth, and because the attack features in published German records.

It is not possible to judge how the raid appeared from the German viewpoint, however. That afternoon's operation had resulted in only a little over half the force despatched finding targets, and as far as can be told, perhaps only eight aircraft actually bombing. It took twenty nine sorties to hit eight targets for the loss of two aircraft.

The bombers that attacked Reading and Newbury had successfully evaded interception over well defended enemy countryside, and the Reading plane appears to have successfully repeated the flight and must be assumed to have returned to its base.

The bombs on Reading hit their target in the most general sense of the term, although, as noted they may not have hit what they were aimed at. As argued above, given the very general aims of German bombing in the west at the time, this was probably quite enough. They may actually have been the only bombs dropped on Reading's built up area to have been aimed at a specific target.

In Reading an individual's experience – and survival – depended on just where they were when. Early closing undoubtedly saved many lives, but plain luck on the day seems to have saved others.

From the point of view of Britain's defences, the bomber had been able to reach its target, and locally, despite extensive preparation, air raid shelters were not used.

The final chapter will look at the immediate aftermath of the raid in Reading.

Chapter Three Notes

1.   Price, Alfred. *Kampfflieger* Vol.3: *Bombers of the Luftwaffe 1942-194*3. Hersham: Classic/Ian allan Publishing, 2005, pp.220.

2.   http://www.ww2.dk/air/kampf/kg40.htm last accessed on 26/12/2015

3.   Philpott, Bryan *The Bombing of Newbury*. Newbury: Pegasus, 1989. P.6-7

4.   Sandall, *Are you 17* p. 142

5.   Philpott, ibid.

6.   Balke, Ulf (1990) *Der Luftkrieg in Europa: Die Operativen Einsatze des Kampgeshwaders 2...Teil 2. Bernard and Graefe Verlag,* Information for 10th February 1943 is pp.197-198.

7.   Price, op cit pp.242 and https://en.wikipedia.org/wiki/Luftflotte_3 Last accessed on 26th March 2016

8.   Max Hastings. *Bomber Command* (Pan, 1979) pp.427.

9.   Philpott op.cit

10. Collier, 1957, pp.512

11. Ibid, Chapters XX and XX1.

12. Manfred Griehl *Do217-317-417: an operational record*. Airlife, 1991 and http://www.warbirdsresourcegroup.org/LRG/do217_variants_E-3_to_E-5.html accessed on 24.09.2015

13. Ibid.

14. Philpott, op.cit. p.13

15. http://www.bmcole.co.uk/coloptics/luftwaffe/A4-READING.htm

16. Balke, op.cit.

17. For an overview of German bomber crew: Stedman, Robert. *Kampfflieger: Bomber crewman of the Luftwaffe 1939-45.* Oxford: Osprey, 2005 (Warrior 99)

18. For references see Chapter 2

19. BRO CD2/3

20. Report of 19th March in National Archives HO192/830

21. Raid Summary RE/B 16/23 2 in National Archives File HO192/830

22. Balke (1990) op.cit.

23. Reported in BRO CD 2/3.

24. Report dated 13th February 1943 in BRO D/EX 1657/2

25. The lecture was on 21st February, with notes in BRO D/EX 1657/2

26. The map is BRO D/EX 1911/1

27. From interview by Mark Bowman, pers. comm. to Author, August 2015

28. Air Raid Damage Region 6 Reading 10.2.43 HO192/830

29. Kelly's Directory 1942

30. Ray Parkes to Author, pers. comm. Jan 20th 2012

31. BRO 1657/2

32. *Reading Chronicle* 8/8/2013 at http://www.readingchronicle.co.uk/news/ retro/13401347.Grandfather__039_s_narrow_escape_in_WW2_bombing/ last accessed on 03/01/2015

Early Closing Day

33.   *Evening Post* 6th December 1999. Clipping in Drury, Colin. *Terror Raid Reading*, 2013

34.   ibid

35.   Raid Summary, op cit

36.   ibid

37.   Ministry of Food. Wartime meals: Summary of ...returns from British Reastauants June 1942-end March 1943. National Archives MAF 99/1749

38.   Measures necessary after heavy air attack Region 6. Jun 1942. (PRO HO 186/931)

39.   *Gloucester Citizen*, 11th February 1943. Accessed online on 25th February 2016

40.   *Portsmouth Evening News* 11th Juanury 1941. Accessed online on 25th February 2016

41.   Collier, Basil *Defence of the United Kingdom*. HMSO, 1957. Appendix XXX.

42.   The advertisement is given in Stuart Hylton *Reading at War*. SEE bibliography.

43.   Holdsworth, Richard. *Six spoons of sugar. Sonning*: Holdsworth Writes, 2008. Pp.1

44.   Rate book for Abbey Ward in BRO at R/FRI/9

45.   Raid summary in PRO HO192/830

46.   ibid

47.   Women's Voluntary Service for Civil Defence Monthly Narrative Report, Reading Centre March 1943.

48.   Letter in *Evening Post* 27th September 1999.

49.   Terry Dezille, pers. Comm. To author, Nov. 2015

50.   ibid

51.   Raid Summary, op.cit

52.   Reading Museum...Summary of interview...20.09.12.

53.   http://www.blandy.co.uk/about/our-history/ Accessed on 05/12/2015

54.   Evening Post 11th February 1969. The author would like to thank Ann Smith for finding the article.

55.   BRO 1657/2

56.   Brian Kite to Author, pers comms. Undated.

57.   http://www.cavershamprimary.org/Mainfolder/PDFs/History/LOG-1938-onwards.pdf accessed on 21 Sept 2012

58.   Peter Seward, pers comm., 30th Jan 2013

59.   Philpott, op.cit.

60.   Mela Fuller on Old Reading Facebook Group, last accessed on 02/01/2016

61.   The War Diary is Foreman, John. *The Fighter Command War Diaries*: January 1942 to June 1943 Vol 3: the Operational History of Fighter Command, Second Tactical Air Force, 100 Group and Air Defence of Great Britain 1939-45. Air Research Publications, 2001. Other references for this section are http://myweb.tiscali.co.uk/609photos/ Snippets.htm and http://www.reading-forum.co.uk/forum/viewtopic.php?f=68&t=714 last accessed on 15.2.13.

13mm German bullet, found in Caversham. Dated 1942, and showing signs that it has been fired, this is almost certainly from one of the German bomber's two MG131 machine guns. (Reading Museum REDMG: 1997.2.106. Copyright Reading Museum (Reading Borough Council. All rights reserved).

Early Closing Day

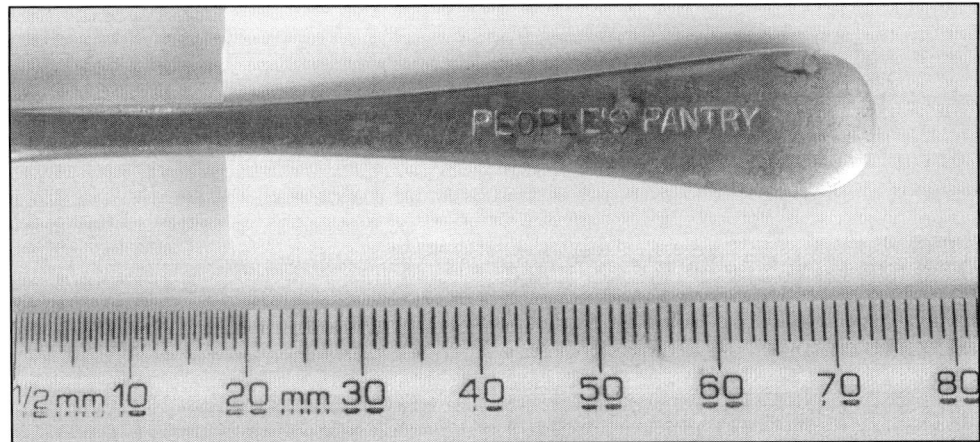

Believed to be one of perhaps two surviving artefacts from the People's Pantry – a teaspoon understood to have been recovered after the attack of 10th February 1943. Note that it is stamped "People's Pantry" on the handle.
Reading Museum REDMG : 2014.7.1.
Copyright Reading Museum (Reading Borough Council). All rights reserved.

Chapter 4
Afterwards
February 1943

Public utilities not seriously affected. No factories involved.
(Home Office Air Raid Damage report, February 1943.)

Depending on the criteria used, the "People's Pantry raid" can be said to have lasted from the moment the aircraft took off, until the time it landed. This, possibly plus planning and debriefing time, marks the duration of that particular operation for the Luftwaffe. For Reading, it was different, and indeed the duration of the incident can be seen as varying with the individual experiences of it.

Given below is a chronology based on official records from the British side. As with the raid on Caversham noted earlier, it shows both confusion over detailed timing, as might be expected when there were more pressing concerns, but also the speed with which civil defence services were able to react. Whilst central control may have been knocked out, individual posts were taking action within minutes of the bombs falling, with additional local resources were being called for around 20 minutes after the first explosion was noted.

An assessment had been made and additional external support had been called for within about 40 minutes and would arrive by around two and half hours after the siren sounded. Apparently anyone who was going to be rescued alive was rescued in under three hours from the alert – although survivors' accounts may suggest otherwise. Perhaps "most people who were to be rescued alive."

Photographic evidence suggest that the rubble had been cleared sufficiently to allow access by at the latest the following morning, in all probability much earlier – Minister Street being cleared within five hours of the second bomb collapsing the rear of Wellsteeds into it. In terms of bare chronology, the immediate aftermath of the raid appeared as follows: [1]

10th February 1943

16.29— Situation report in PRO from 11th says Red alert

16.32 – A Group (HQ Surley Row) reports alarm to Chief Warden

16.33 – KG2 war diary report say bombs dropped

16.34 – Post D5 (Market Place) reports HE bombs on Arcade/Friar St

16.35 – Post E2 (Hope Street/Soho Street) reports need for rubble baskets to

Early Closing Day

help in rescue work

16.35 — Group B (Tilehurst Triangle) reports plane machine gunned Cold Storage Depot

16.36 – D5 reports HE bombs in Minster St

16.38 – F Group HQ in East St report sirens

16.44 – F Group report Air Raid Warning Red

16.50 - F Group report bombs

16.52 – F Group say can't raise Control Centre

16.55 – Post E2 reports need for ambulance at H. G. Simmonds, 32 Broad Street.

16.58 – Additional Rescue Party requested

17.00 – E2 reports/requests an ambulance at Simond's First Air Post, Fobney Street. – WVS mobile trailer canteen in place

        - US Military Police arrive

17.02 – Additional rescue party requested (in addition to 16.58)

17.08—Situation report in PRO say White Alert

17.10 - Regional reinforcements requested

17.20 – Additional Rescue Party requested

17.25 – F Group report casualties in London St – refugees from Market Place

17.30 – F Group send wardens to town centre

17.50 – F Group report 3 casualties at 29 London St.

18.00 – F Group report wardens managing traffic in Duke St, windows broken in Southampton St and wardens clearing glass.

18.20 – F Group report neighbours missing from Silver St

19.00 - Regional reinforcements arrive

c. 1900 – All trapped people rescued [2]

20.00 – Report and Control Centre moved to Whitley Rise.

21.00 – E Group report a rescue party sent to the Arcade

22.20 – E Group report Minster St cleared

22.20 – E Group say troops from Pay Corps relieved by Home Guard

Rest Centres open night 10/11th – Oxford Hall

Admin/Information centres open

Two of three incidents closed.

11th February

Casualty Bureau open with full list ready "by daybreak"

More US troops arrive

Rifle Brigade and Royal Engineers arrive

Part time first aid drivers off duty

08.00 - "Searcher Service" – closes evening 15th with 54 enquires

    Most incidents closed

    Shadow Information Centre open at Town Hall

14.00 – E Group say still unidentified bodies at Sackville Street mortuary

14th February

Special constables stood down having been on duty since 10 Feb.

15th February

Administration/information centres close

16th February

Shadow information centre closes 17.30

Last fatally injured casualty dies in hospital.

Funerals of casualties of 10th.

17th Feb

US troops, Royal Engineers and Rifle Brigade leave

20th February

WVS canteens come off duty

22nd February

Blankets sent by the Queen for "those who had suffered most"

27th February

WVS box cycle canteen off duty

Early Closing Day

Over Reading, the raid lasted, officially, from "Red Alert" to "All Clear". Everything else belonged to a new phase, that of incident managment, rescue and repair. Using this timing, the attack of 10th February lasted from 1629 to 17.08, just under half an hour.

The main "incident" – that caused by the bombs on the People's Pantry and Town Hall - was closed at about half past five on February 16th when the shadow information centre opened.   The last official action – before the process of reporting and learning began – came with the final withdrawal of the Women's Voluntary Service whose members had been providing refreshments for the civil defence from a matter of minutes after the bombs fell.[3]

Taken in a wider perspective, the work done in oral history, and simply in chatting to people who witnessed this raid, shows that in a sense, the events are still "live".   However, for the purposes of this account, this chapter will be confined to the immediate aftermath of the February 10th raid and will look at the Civil Defence reaction and the actual damage inflicted.

People

Derek Chamberlain remembered that he woke up surrounded by rubble next to an old lady. Afterwards he was told that he's been blown all the way back to the Broad Street entrance of the Arcade. Interviewed in 2012, he recalled hearing noises – taps dripping, gas, concrete falling. The lady beside him said 'What has happened to us?'.   Later she told his mother that Derek replied 'It doesn't matter Lady, It'll be alright'.[4]

Peter Prest, then nine, may have walked past Derek Chamberlain as he waited for his friend. Mr Prest and his friend had just had a mug of tea each in the People's Pantry – it cost them a penny each – and were walking for the bus home to Caversham. They had just got as far as Station Road when the bombs fell. In 2013 Peter Prest recalled:

We didn't know what the hell it was. It perforated my eardrum. There was debris, bricks and smoke everywhere. Everybody was screaming and yelling.[5]

Alan Sandall – author of *Are You 17*, in which he gives a fictionalised account of his time in Reading's Auxiliary Fire Service – was working as a reporter for the *Reading Standard*. That tea-time, he had just turned into Valpy Street towards the *Standard's* office , putting the Town Hall between him and the bombs when he hear the aircraft and the first bomb to fall. He turned back and went to the scene.

Writing in 2013, he gave one of the few first hand written accounts of the immediate aftermath of the third and fourth bombs to fall.[6]

Outside the Town Hall...and through the Arcade and Market Place,
it was a scene of carnage, bloodied bodies, teetering buildings and the roar
of a gas main flamed into the air at Blandy's...one or more were trapped
in the solicitor's office but when we realised it was a gas main we [the firemen]
let it burn and kept watch [as] extinguished leaking gas could have exploded...All
though the Market Place and down into Minster Street all I could see was one big
pile of rubble.

Over the road from the Town Hall, and a few yards away from Derek Chamberlain, Michael Bond, later author of the Paddington Bear stories was working in the BBC "H" transmitting station on the top floor of 175 Friar St.

The H transmitter network was set up to re-broadcast important information in the event that national transmitters were overrun or hit. Significantly for accounts suggesting that the transmitter was specifically targeted, Michael Bond noted that it was turned off whenever enemy aircraft approached.

In his autobiography he recalls that the bomb blew out the floors below the transmitter, and that he and his colleagues had to climb down what was left of the stairs. In the remains of the building he encountered a girl with both legs blown off and a hand "clutching a pair of false teeth".[7]

An unpublished photograph from the *Reading Chronicle's* archive shows a large tabby cat apparently rescued from the roof of 175 Friar Street.[8]

According to her daughter, the last person to be rescued alive from the People's Pantry was Mrs G.A.Nickler, who was in charge of catering, and who was rescued at about 10pm.[9] Mrs Nickler was taken to the Royal Berkshire Hospital on a United States army jeep having been rescued by a Mr H. F Skidmore of the St John's Ambulance. (According to Emergency and Invasion Committee minutes, for 27th April 1943 Mr Skidmore was the County ARP Officer of the Berkshire St John's Ambulance – a reminder of the widespread involvement of voluntary and charitable organisations outside the formal civil defence structure).

Meeting on the 13th February, the Emergency and Invasion Committee, made provision for the funerals of "persons who had been killed as a result of the

Early Closing Day

attack and for whose interment the Corporation had been requested to be responsible": 10.00 on the 16th at Henley Road Municipal Cemetery.[10]

The picture of the human cost changed over time. The Air Raid Damage report, written on the 11th said 32 had been killed,[11] but papers in the same file refer to 35 killed with 42 seriously injured and 72 lightly injured. By the 13th February, this had risen to 42 killed, 51 seriously injured and 77 lightly injured, with 80% of the casualties in the People's Pantry.[12]

Reading's own report on the incident gave 192 casualties overall, 41 killed, with 35 in the People's Pantry. The *Berkshire Chronicle* listed dead and injured but its report was censored[13] – indeed according to the paper in 2000, even death notices were censored. The censored copy – or at least part of it – survives, and at the time it was written, 10 people had still to be identified – six men and four women. This must date the list to not long after the raid, probably having been taken from the list compiled by the Casualty Bureau on the night of 10th-11th February.

The report includes around forty names for those taken to hospital – these are given where legible in Appendix 2. Included in the list is Derek Chamberlain.

The names of 37 people killed on 10th February are known, and these are given in an appendix. Two unidentified bodies are buried in the Henley Road Cemetery.

This leaves the obvious question of how the figure of 41 was arrived at, and how accurate it was. Contemporary records cast no light on this, but the Reading Corporation ARP services were best placed to know. Could it simply be that an additional two people were so mutilated as to produce no buriable remains?

The Commonwealth War Graves Commission entries for the dead allow a general statistical picture to be constructed.[14] Of the 39 given, 36 were killed on 10th February, three injured later died in hospital.

At least 29 people were killed or fatally injured in the People's Pantry, with four at 29 Market Place and two in the Arcade. Three were killed either in Market Street or Market Place.

Two people were killed either in or outside the Town Hall, one in Blandy and Blandy's.

Two died in Minster Street, with another in Broad St.

As mentioned in Chapter 3 it is not possible to separate the dead for the People's Pantry incident by the bomb which killed them, as the pair fell so close together, but it does seem likely that most of those killed were killed by a single bomb.

The ages of those killed reflect a town where most adults of working age were either engaged in war work or in the Forces. The oldest person killed was 75 year old Ellen Simmonds, the youngest were two ten year olds, Violet Brown and George Langford from Salcombe Road in Whitley who was killed in the People's Pantry.

Twenty-one of the dead were over 50 – the average age of a victim was 48. Fifteen were female.

Most of those killed lived in Reading, although four people from outside the town were killed – one each from Wokingham, Bracknell, Aldershot and Southampton.

Nellie Dixon, killed in the People's Pantry, was 28, and came from County Wexford in the Republic of Ireland.

63 year old Aristide Maccrini (also given as Maccarini) lived in London Street but was an Italian national. He was killed at the off-licence at 29 Market Place.

From the Commonwealth War Graves Commission information, 79 UK civilians died as a result of enemy action on 10th February 1943, just under 300 were to die in February that year.

Raids on Chichester and Newbury on the afternoon of 10th February killed 18 and 15 respectively.[15]

At least eight German aircrew died that afternoon over Britain.

Civil Defence

The "White Alert" – the "all clear" was sounded at 17.08.[16]

The Situation Report has the Red Alert, the actual warning being given at 16.29. Accounts from Reading put the fall of bombs and the sound of the sirens as almost simultaneous -, although the wardens service F Group headquarters in East St did not log the alert until 16.44 with the sirens being heard six minutes earlier.[17]

The difference in timing may be frustrating to a later historian, but on the ground on that day it can have made little difference, as by the nature of the attack, civil defence services were on the scene at once.

The nearest Wardens Posts were D5 – the Headquarters of D Group – directly in the path of the third bomb in a basement in Market Passage, now Market Way,

Early Closing Day

and the E Group posts in Hope Street and Wolseley Street which were close to the Minister Street bombs.

Apart from Royal Berkshire Hospital, the nearest first aid post was in the Silver St.

D5 was knocked out by the bomb, and yet still managed to report in, as mentioned above, reporting both its own and the Minister St bombs.

The Report and Control Centre was a matter of feet from the fourth bomb, and was effectively put out of operation- at 16.52 F Group tried to make contact and failed.

It seems that the Centre – or at least parts of its team – were still capable of responding. The Centre remained in operation until eight o'clock when it moved to the alterative centre at Whitley Rise, and police constables were used to pass messages from Chief Constable to the ARP controller. .

Mr R. Ladd worked as the Town Clerk's Secretary, and knew the Report and Control Centre, and its staff, personally. He was interviewed in the 1990s by Reading Museum.[18]

Mr Ladd recalled that the Civil Defence Committee met in the Assistant Solicitor's office off the entrance to the large Town Hall. The main Control Room – under direction of Mr W.A. Smallcombe was in the basement which was reinforced with timbers. A semi basement ran parallel to Blagrave Street. A blast wall was built outside the entrance next to St Laurence's church.

The Town Clerk's office was badly damaged, the Town Clerk "shaken up" and Deputy Town Clerk, Mr Porter had to send him home and take over.

Mr Ladd's wife, Kay, worked in the Report Centre with Joan Thackery who was fatally injured.

On the alarm, Mrs Ladd and others were going to take shelter but with no sense of urgency. Miss Thackery was on way to the door when she was hit by flying debris propelled along the corridor by the fourth bomb. Mrs Ladd was injured and shocked.

In 1969 Kay Ladd gave one of a very few comments dealing directly with the German aircrew – although a number of people recalled seeing the faces of the men in the Dornier, none of the contemporary accounts used here record any feelings at all about the Germans — *Afterwards we hated his guts, but he was only doing his job – the same as ours were doing to his country.*[19]

Writing after the war, Lord Baler of Windrush, who led the Ministry of Home

Chapter 4

Security's Research and Experiments Branch, was harsh in his criticism of design flaws in the added protection provided for the Town Hall.[20] Describing the effects as "almost comic" he pointed out that the blast wall that had been hurled into the corridor into which Miss Thackery had just stepped had not been reinforced – it was simply a 3 foot wall of 18inch hollow blocks – and the strengthening done to the passage itself had not been joined to the structure of the floor or ceiling. The result was that the combination of blocks from outside and strengthening posts caused what Lord Baker called "a mammoth game of skittles".

Mr Ladd recalled in his interview with the Museum, that the Borough Surveyor Mr Parsons was upset as it was said that there was no blast wall, and he had only been asked to "do a gas curtain".

Brian Fowles was a messenger in the Report and Control Centre. Interviewed in 2012 he told Stuart Hylton —

He was then sixteen years old. In addition to his apprenticeship with the gas company, he was a volunteer Civil Defence messenger. The Report Centre dealing with civil defence was in the basement of the Town Hall. One night each week he and several other volunteer messengers stayed overnight in the Town Hall basement, ready to deliver messages as required. The Head of ARP was a Mr Gilmore, (the Deputy Town Clerk?).

On the day of the raid, he was at work when he heard the alarm and immediately set off on his bicycle for the Town Hall. Near the top of Market Place, he heard (but did not see) the bomber, which was flying at low altitude, machine gunning as it went. Then he saw a man lying on the pavement, apparently hit by falling masonry. He leapt from his bicycle to help him but was blown off his feet by the force of an explosion. He has no recollection of hearing an explosion. The next thing he remembered was lying on the step of the small Town Hall, having been blown by the force of the blast some sixteen yards. Miraculously, he was completely unhurt. Had he got there a moment earlier, he would probably have been under the falling masonry himself. In the confusion of the moment, he forgot about the man on the pavement and made his way into the Town Hall, to offer his services as a messenger. Not surprisingly, the Town Hall telephones were out of order due to bomb damage and, about half an hour later, he was sent over to the Market Place to try and find Mr Gilmore. The police were by now holding back crowds of sightseers, but let him through.

His bicycle was lying abandoned among the debris and he later went to

Early Closing Day

> retrieve it. It had suffered only bent mudguards and broken spokes. He took
> it to a bicycle repair shop and the Council reimbursed him the 15s (75p)
> cost of the repairs.[21]

Brian Fowles was commended in writing by the Chief Warden in his report on the raid.

Messenger Fowles – This boy is one of the report centre messengers... [he] was in Mill Lane at the time of the alert. He left for the Town Hall and, being in the vicinity when the bombs exploded, was twice thrown by the blast...He nevertheless reported for duty and remained until 19.30 hours.[22]

In 2015, Peggy Stanlake remembered -

> *I immediately went to town, being a warden I felt I should. I lived in*
> *St John's Road only a short walk to town. The place was littered with glass!*
> *I was told to go home, I wasn't needed.*
> *I do remember seeing a sight in Walkers or Home and Colonial shop,*
> *the one at Broad Street end of the arcade. This shop had a sloping marble front*
> *and on it was a huge container of that yellow pickle and mustard and bits of*
> *vegetables were slipping down the shop front (minus the glass). Real horror!*
> *I hate pickles and mustard.*
> *As I walked back home, Kings Road was gridlocked with American*
> *jeeps ferrying wounded people to Watlington Street and to the Royal Berks.*
> *Faces covered in blood which was caused by many fragments of glass, I was told.*

Pat Barker, then Pat Mery, who was 17 at the time, arrived in Reading on the 16.50 from Paddington. She had a job in London. Interviewed in 2015, she remembered *a sea of fire hoses and fire engines outside Reading General.* [24]

She had no Idea of what had happened until she got home. Her mother told her that a relative, Laurence Yaxley was blown through a glass door in the Town Hall and injured.

If Mrs Barker recalled that evening correctly, she adds an interesting detail as she remembered walking up to Broad Street to catch the trolleybus - Route A - to Wokingham Road. If this is so, Broad Street must have been cleared within an hour of the bombing. Ray Smith and John Whitehead, in their history of Reading Buses in the war years suggest buses may have been running at some point soon afterwards, at least in one direction.

A trolleybus which was stationary near Wellsteeds, suffered splinter damage and was left covered in dust and surrounded by shoes that had been blown out of

Mansfield's shop on the corner of Minster Street by the second bomb.[25]

Despite the fact that their office had been wrecked the WVS had a "box tricycle" (possibly a converted ice cream sellers bike) in place by five o'clock, following it up with Ford food vans.

As noted in Chapter 1, WVS workers brought the British Restaurants in Kings Road and Oxford Road into operation, providing food and drinks for the rescue teams.

In the report on the raid, two main criticisms were made. First, there proved to be a shortage of wardens in the town centre, and second that people simply got in the way of the civil defence services. The first point was a function of the linkage of number of wardens to number of people – there were very few people actually living in the town centre, and hence only a single Warden's Post.

Alongside this, action was taken to increase stretcher bearers available at the Royal Berkshire Hospital, suggesting that this may have proved inadequate to deal with the sudden volume of wounded.[26]

Commendations given to individual members of the ARP services, and contained in the Chief Warden's account, show individual vignettes of the period immediately after the bombing.[27]

Party Supervisor CS Barrett, Foxley Depot – was overcome by coal gas but returned to work at the People's Pantry and continued on duty until after midnight

Senior Warden Cross – He was the only warden on duty at D group headquarters [Market Place] and although affected by the explosion of a bomb he managed to sum up the situation and go to the Report Centre to give a message to the Deputy Controller.

Miss Macrini – She is a full time ambulance driver at the Castle depot. She was off duty and out of Reading when she returned she was informed that her father was a fatal casualty. Nevertheless the following morning she reported for duty and carried out a trying task throughout the day although every effort was made to persuade her to go off duty.

(Miss Macrini's Father was killed in or outside 29 Market Place, most probably by the third bomb to fall. He was 53)

The Town Hall was brought back into operation on the 22nd February with a blast wall of sandbags in the corridor where Joan Thackery had been fatally injured.[28]

Early Closing Day

What appears from the official reports is a picture of a set of structures working in very much the way they had been designed to.

Certainly, this was the view at the time. On the 22nd February, the Emergency and Invasion Committee recorded the thanks of the Commandant of the Regional Mobile Column (designed to offer rapid reinforcements to anywhere attacked) for "messing facilities afforded" and his approval of the work done and cooperation locally, and Reading's civil defence services passed inspection by the Ministry of Home Security four months later.

Depots at Castle Hill and Foxley had first aid parties and ambulances on site within ten minutes. All first aid post except Grovelands (of the "Town" posts the furthest from the scene) took in casualties, spreading the load just as they had been designed to. Most went to the Royal Berkshire Hospital and to the First Aid Post in Silver Street. Temporary first aid posts were set up in police buildings.

The dead were moved to three mortuaries, and extra staff brought in from Oxford and Maidenhead on the 12th February to relieve the Reading staff.

Emergency and Invasion Committee minutes from the time seem to suggest a renewed interest in public shelters after 10th February 1943, but it is not clear if this was a direct result of the raid, or a return to the completion of a pre existing scheme. However, the discussion of keeping public shelters unlocked at this time certainly seems connected.

Damage to Buildings

The Dornier's payload had directly hit three buildings, struck three others and blast from the fourth bomb to fall had seriously damaged three more.

Contemporary written accounts of the damage are limited, but photographic evidence shows that the damage in Minster Street and Friar Street in particular was localised, but severe, and secondary damage was much more widespread, especially if the effects of machine gun fire are included.

The bombs broke windows in London Street and Mill Lane, and most probably in many other locations across the centre of town. In St Mary's Church the Diary and Service Book recorded that the:

East Window was slightly and the windows of the Lady Chapel more extensively broken by blast.[29]

In the other direction, across the Forbury Gardens from St Laurence's, blast damaged St James' Church.[30]

Chapter 4

This section will give a sketch of the main focus of the damage.

The Corporation was responsible for listing any buildings "damaged as to be beyond repair or likely to be unsafe" and under the guidance of the Borough Surveyor began its formal inspections on the 18th February.

Wellsteeds

Wellsteed's Broad Street., February 1943
In the left hand image, the damage is more apparent. In the right hand image, taken about a week after the raid, rubble has been cleared,. At right, the sign for Wellsteed's basement shelter can be seen. (Left hand image, Reading Libraries, right Roger Peacock collection via Reading Libraries 1392091)

Although the frontage on Broad Street appears in good condition in contemporary photographs, the rear of Wellsteeds was effectively wrecked. About a third was actually demolished by the SC500, perhaps another quarter or third badly damaged.

A plan drawn up for insurance purposes in 1943, and a partner from 1944 show the rear as about to be demolished or unfit for use, although by 1944 the Ministry of Works had moved into the Broad Street side of the building, leaving Wellsteeds with a short ground floor stretch on Broad Street.

In May 1943 the Emergency and Invasion Committee heard that damage to the *Western wall of Wellsteeds' main building [prevented] use of the yard behind the Cheddar Cheese and of a three storey building by Messers Watsons [as they were] threatened by an overhanging portion of the wall*

Interviewed in 2000, Colin Blackburn, who was eight at the time, recalled that

Early Closing Day

when rubble from the bombed building was dumped at the "old fairground" site in Great Knollys Street, it was found to contain talcum powder and jars of face cream, which he and his friends assumed came from Wellsteeds.[31]

Wellsteeds moved out to premises in 7-10 St Mary's Butts with a store at 11 Cork Street.[32]

Minster St, February 1943. By contrast, at the rear most of the Minster Street side of Wellsteeds, and much of Saunder's next door was demolished. The glass dome of the restaurant is visible just left of centre. Reading's Civil Defence services noted that the 500kg bomb had been fitted with a short delay fuse. This meant that it did not detonate until it was actually inside Wellsteed's maximising the effect of its explosive filling.

(Reading Libraries 1392075)

The People's Pantry, looking towards Market Place, probably on 11th February 1943. Although by 1943 Civil Defence services had considerable experience of dealing with bomb damage, this was the most severe incident to hit Reading. The complexity of the task, especially given the lack of knowledge of just who might have been in the building, is readily apparent. (Reading Libraries)

People's Pantry and Arcade

All that remains of the People's Pantry today are some fragments of tile and a spoon in Reading Museum.

By VE day - over two years later – photographs of the area show that the building, and most of the arcade next door, had been largely demolished, and both the 1947 Goad Insurance Plan held in Reading Library and an aerial photograph from 1946 show a blank area stretching almost back to Broad Street.

The town's other British Restaurants – which seldom feature in memories – took over the work, and once the rubble had been cleared the site remained empty until the Bristol & West arcade was built in the late 1950s.[33] The People's Pantry re-opened in Cross Street in 1944 or 45, finally closing in 1951[34] The idea of British Restaurants was revived, briefly, by the Civic Restaurants Act of 1947, but the network itself did not survive.[35]

On the ground, the "new" building line of the Arcade steps back from six to about fifteen feet from the original, so part of the area of the People's Pantry is – at the time of writing – open pavement. In 2012 the area became the focus of a £450,000 improvement plan but redevelopment of the Bristol and West Arcade, which had been discussed since at least 2005 has yet to happen. [36]

Access to Broad Street from Friar Street through Sainsbury's follows the general line of the Victorian arcade demolished in February 1943.

Tenders for the actual demolition of 173 and 174 Friar Street were received by the Corporation in June 1943, with the work given to the Reading Demolition Company for £940.

St Laurence's

St Laurence's Church may be the only building in Reading directly to bear scars from the Germans bombs of 1943. Photographs taken the day after the raid show pock marks from splinters that are still in the stonework today.

Although the basic structure of the frontage of the Church was left in place – like that of the Town Hall and other buildings around the location of the third and fourth bombs - St Laurence's was extensively damaged.

A claim for £551/10 was put in under the War Damage Act 1941, and assessed by the War Damage Commission's Regional Office at Coley Park.[37]

Early Closing Day

Splinter damage to St Laurence's Church, 2008. Possibly the most immediate evidence of the 1943 raid still visible. (Author's photograph)

Internal damage included damage to the heating, lighting, St John's Chapel, Nave and screens.

The whole vestry had to be pulled down, and stained glass had to be replaced by clear glass. The restored vestry was rededicated in October 1950.[38]

On the tower, feet away from the explosion, the pinnacles had to be removed, with the work undertaken in April 1943.[39] A claim was put in to replace the pinnacles with crosses and a weather vane. As is evident today, this was never done.

Services at the Church resumed on the 2nd June.[40]

Blandy and Blandy's – No 1 Friar Street.

Blandy and Blandy's Victorian Gothic building at 1 Friar Street had its front demolished by the fourth SC500. Photographs taken before WW2 show an elaborate building, whose frontage was wrecked and dumped into the street outside.

The firm's first move was to a temporary office at 8 The Forbury, and in photographs taken on VE Day and after the war the Friar Street front of their offices appears covered in tarpaulins and battens.

The office was finally rebuilt in the early 1950s, and took its present form in the 1990s. Damage to the Town Hall put temporary Corporation offices in the garden. These were later taken over by Blandy's and finally demolished in 1999 to make way for a new extension.[41]

As discussed below, Blandy's generously offered their wall, as well as financial support to the memorial of the victims of the bombing that destroyed their offices.

Town Hall

Demolition removed the rear of Wellsteeds, all the Arcade and the People's Pantry but the Town Hall retained signs of what had happened at tea time on 10th February for many years.

The south tower and most of the frontage between the tower and Blandy and Blandy's was reduced to rubble by the force of the explosion. In post war photographs the roof line shows as dramatically changed by the demolition of the tower, although below roof level reconstruction returned much of the Victorian appearance.

The building as a whole survived discussion of complete redevelopment in the early 1970s, and the tower was finally rebuild with extensive grants in 1988-89 as part of overall work to refurbish the Town Hall.[42]

Plan of damage to Wellsteed's, February 1943. Drawn up for insurance purposes, this shows the situation a week after the raid. The rear of the store is shown in yellow as "demolished" with only the front, shown in red, slightly damaged.
(Roger Peacock Collection via Reading Libraries 1392022)

Early Closing Day

Conclusion

It is hard to assess the damage to Reading and the response of the civil defence services objectively.

For anyone with a close association with the town, the photographs of the aftermath of the raid and descriptions of the damage done are shocking.

Where damage occurred, it and loss of life was severe, but limited. Although windows were shattered and injuries were sustained from broken glass hundreds of yards from the bombs, and buildings were damaged by machine gun fire over a mile away, the actual area of the attack was limited to a strip perhaps only around a hundred yards long.

This is not to minimise the effect of the raid on the families of those killed, those injured and those who lost businesses and livelihoods as a result, but, whilst it may seem harsh, the Home Office report quoted at the start of this chapter was correct – KG40 had hit nothing of direct importance to the war effort.

Furthermore, although worked enormously hard, the small scale of the incident and the localised extent of the damage put it well within the means of Reading's civil defence, supported with regional forces, to cope with. There were problems, but nothing that stopped casualties being treated and risks contained.

One aspect of the raid – indeed of all the raids on Reading – that is impossible to gauge is the psychological impact on those witnessing, if not actually directly affected by, the events. We live in a time when individual and collective psychological well being is closely attended to, and it is recognised that events, ranging from terrorist attacks to natural disasters will cause suffering beyond the physical damage done. In the Second World War it was recognised at a national level that there would be psychological casualties from air attack, yet these are nowhere directly referred to in the papers from civil defence in Reading. People may be described as "nervous" or "shaken" and provision was made for rest centres, but even in survivors' accounts there is little to show what impact bombing had on people's minds.

Talking to a range of individuals who were in Reading that Wednesday afternoon, it is clear that it is something that they will never forget, but beyond this it is hard to judge its effects.

Part of the next section will examine how the town has remembered the air raid on 10th February 1943 and how the events have moved from direct experience to community memory.

VE day, May 1945.
Behind the Naval veterans marching past, the walls of the People's
Pantry and Arcade have been reduced to a stub and the West Window
of St Laurence's, which took the force of the fourth bomb just yards
away, still appear to be boarded over.
(Reading Libraries 1267044)

Interior of the Town Hall, February 1943.
On the first floor looking towards the Arcade and People's Pantry. The window has
been blown in, but there is surprisingly little visible damage otherwise.
(Reading Libraries)

Early Closing Day

The Town Hall, Blandy's, St Laurence's and the People's Pantry, February 11th 1943

Images taken the following morning showing Civil Defence workers and military personnel on site, with a route through the rubble cleared and work still in progress, by this stage to make the buildings safe and recover any dead. The smoke is possibly from a ruptured gas main, allowed to burn to prevent a build up of fumes.

Although the exact time isn't known, given that it is daylight on a February morning, the situation would be under the control of the Report and Control Centre at Whitley Rise and an Information Centre would be open in the Town Hall itself, with a "Searcher Service" giving and taking details of missing people.

The National Fire Service turntable ladder seen here was one of the first vehicles on the scene and was later used to remove the damaged pinnacles of St Laurence's.

The damage seen here around the Town Hall, Blandy's and St Laurence's was mostly caused by the fourth bomb dropped, and represents the effects of 220 kilos – 484lbs of high explosive going off within about 30 feet of the buildings.
(Reading Libraries)

Early Closing Day

Sections of the 1941 and 1947 Goad Insurance Plans of Reading town centre, showing, below, the Minster Street area and top the area of the Arcade and People's Pantry in 1941 and 1947, before and after the raid of February 1943. Note the demolition work that had taken place by the time of the 1947 plans as a result of the 1943 bombing. (Reading Libraries. Photographs by Richard Marks).

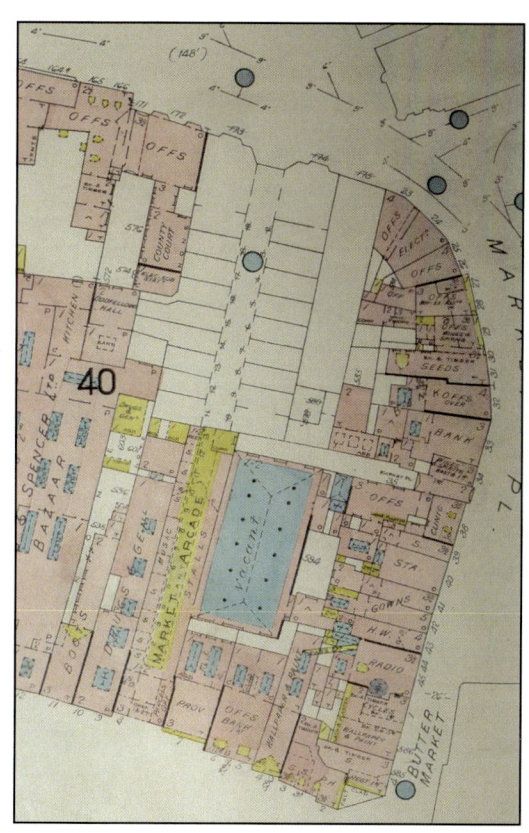

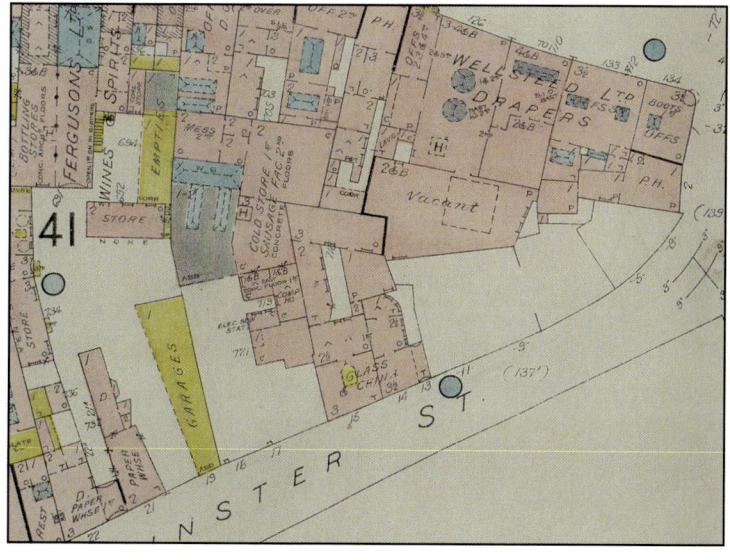

Early Closing Day

Aerial photograph of central Reading, 1949.
St Laurence's is just to the left of centre, with the flattened area of the
arcade leading towards Broad St just opposite.
(Reading Libraries 1405987)

Chapter Four Notes

1. The main source for this, and much of the detail in this section is Report on enemy air attack on 10 February 1943 in BRO D/EX/1657/2
2. The time is that given in the official papers, but according to a letter given in Colin Drury's *Terror Raid Reading*, the last person to be rescued alive from the People's Pantry was Mrs G.A.Nickler who was in charge of catering, and who was rescued at about 10pm
3. Women's Voluntary Service for Civil Defence Monthly Narrative Report, Reading Centre March 1943
4. Reading Museum...Summary of interview...20.09.12.
5. http://www.getreading.co.uk/news/local-news/bomb-survivor-peoples-pantry-ceremony-4192067 last accessed on 03/01/2015
6. Pers comm to the author, 10/2/2013
7. Bond, Michael. *Bears and forebears: A Life so far*. London, Harper Collins, 1996 pp.74-76. There is an audio interview with Michael bond at http://www.readingmuseum.org.uk/news/2012/jan/paddington-bear-writer-reading-podcast-online/ (Accessed 28/12/2015). A brief note on the H transmitters is given at https://en.wikipedia.org/wiki/BBC_Home_Service (last accessed 18/12/2015)
8. Reading Museum object number REDMG : 1980.36.A570.7 Accessed online on 20th February 2016
9. Notes and undated cutting in Drury, Colin. *Terror Raid Reading*, 2013. The note is a letter from Mrs Nickler's daughter
10. Committee Minutes, 13/2/1943
11. National Archives HO/192/830
12. BRO D/EX 1657/2
13. Midweek Chronicle, 200. Undated cutting in Drury, op.cit.
14. http://www.cwgc.org/find-war-dead.aspx last accessed on 03/01/2016
15. The author's thanks go to Ken Green for kindly supplying a text of his booklet *Second World War Bombing of Chichester* (Chichester Local History Group, 2012.
16. National Archives HO192/830
17. BRO D/EX 1657/2
18. Reading Museum Oral History interview Oral History Interview 22 part 1Ref 1997.127.22
19. *Evening Post* 11th February 1969
20. Baker. *Enterprise versus Bureaucracy*. p.19
21. Stuart Hylton pers comm to Author, 8˙10. 2012
22. From BRO D/LY/1657/2
23. Interview with Mark Bowman, Pers Comm to Author Augusr 2015
24. Neil Barker, pers.comm. to author 3/1/2016
25. Ray Smith and John Whitehead *War and austerity*. Reading: Millane Publishing. 2014. Pp. 72
26. Committee minutes 18th February 1943.

Early Closing Day

27. BRO D/LY/1657/2 op cit
28. Committee Minutes 19th February 1943
29. BRO D/P98/1B/2
30. In the other direction, across the Forbury from St Laurence's , it appears likely that damage understood to have happened at St James' Church also happened at this time. Mike Keep. Pers.Comm to the Author, 17th March 2016.
31. Drury, Colin. Terror Raid Reading, 2013
32. Committee Minutes 17/8/1943
33. Reading Corporation Town Planning and Building Committee Minutes, 13 November 1944 and Hylton, Stuart. *Reading 1800 to the present day*. Pp.97
34. Hylton, Stuart, *Reading in the 1950s*, Sutton 2013 p.67.
35. https://en.wikipedia.org/wiki/British_Restaurant last accessed 11th February 2016
36. http://www.reading.gov.uk/pressreleases/2012/sep/450-000-improvement-to-town-hall-square/ last accessed on 12th April 2013
37. BRO D/P97/8A/18
38. *Berkshire Chronicle* 16 October 1950, quoted in the caption to Reading Museum object number REDMG : 1980.36.B290.5. Accessed online on 20/2/2016
39. Committee Minutes 2nd April 1943. A Caption to a photograph in Alan Sandall *Are you 17*. (1993) may suggest that the NFS was involved in this. Committee Minutes 2nd June 1943
40. http://www.blandy.co.uk/about/our-history/ accessed 21/12/2015.
41. *Evening Post* 17/1/19179 and 13/7/1988 and *Reading Chronicle* 24/11/1989.

The Town Hall and Blandy and Blandy's, 1950.
Blandy's is still boarded over, and the roofline of the Town Hall been changed by the demolition of the upper part of the south tower.
(Reading Libraries 1287892)

Chapter 5
Remembering

The previous chapter looked at how the bombing raid on 10th February 1943 changed parts of Reading, mainly in Minster Street and near the Town Hall.

However, it is clear that the raid left other traces in the way the town remembered, and still remembers, World War Two.

Newspaper coverage of the bombing of the People's Pantry began within less than 24 hours. As this happened, so three distinct strands of information about the event were created.

The first of these was the official, unpublished records. These have been used extensively here, and were being created during and immediately after the event as part of the routine bureaucracy of civil defence

The second was the published record. In effect wartime censorship meant that this was another form of official record, but it was created with an entirely different purpose, to inform but especially to shape opinion. "News management" was not a creation of the 1990s. The Ministry of Information approved, released or held back information to suit national policy, and it was able to affect the published news record down to local level.

The creation of "news" also played a role in the final strand, the creation of a popular account and popular memory of events. People witnessed the events of 10th February, they talked to other people about them (or didn't, depending on their role in them and how seriously they took "careless talk"). People also read newspaper accounts then and subsequently, and passed those on to others.

The local newspapers covered the events of 10th February later that week, and although Reading was identified only as a "Home Counties town", the text and photographs would have left no-one with any knowledge of Reading in any doubt as to the location of the bombing.[1]

In the *Berkshire Chronicle* considerable detail was given — for example mention of Clarence Brown who survived the Minster Street bomb — with descriptions of the damage from each of the bombs, but stressing continuity of "business as usual", to use the paper's phrase.

Reading was not identified by its own newspapers as the target until May 1943. The *Reading Mercury* identified the People's Pantry for the first time in a feature on VE Day, run in May 1945.[2]

Early Closing Day

However, the story was in the national papers the following day, and had also reached local papers elsewhere. For example, although not actually identified, the People's Pantry appeared in coverage of the previous day's raids in the *Daily Herald* on February 11th. The paper gave an overview of damage to a number of towns – anonymised as, for example, "Town B" – but led its account of the "cloud-hopping" raid with a description of work to rescue those trapped in what, again to anyone with any knowledge of the town, was clearly Reading. The *Herald* noted damage to "an old church and a Labour Hall" as well as to the British Restaurant.

Given the time needed to produce a morning edition, the story must have reached the *Daily Herald* at some point on the night of 10th-11th February at the latest, and most probably originated with the Ministry of Information.

The *Daily Telegraph* included very similar phrases

RESTAURANT AND SCHOOL HIT
Cloud-hopping raiders, following their now familiar fanning –out tactics, attacked nearly 20 towns and villages in South – East England and the Home Counties shortly before dusk yesterday. Three were brought down out of a force which is believed not to have exceeded 10.
One crashed in flames on open land near a large hotel at Saltdean, between Newhaven and Brighton. It had been attacking agricultural villages and machine – gunning cattle. All three of the crew were killed.
A second, a Dornier 217, was brought down near Bognor. It barely cleared the houses before crashing into a field.
The third, a Messerschmitt 109 fighter – bomber, was shot down into the Channel by a Typhoon after a chase a few feet above the sea off Dover. Everywhere the raiders were met by heavy gunfire.

as did the *Daily Mail* – the reference here is not to Reading:

Channel Chase
But in one town a fighter – bomber returned after being driven off and dropped a bomb next door to a large store which was packed with market – day crowds. Casualties were not known late last night...

One of the raiders crashed in flames near a large hotel at Saltdean, Sussex. Another was reported to have been brought down near Bognor. The third was shot down after a Channel chase by Typhoons.

As discussed in Chapter 3, the aircraft shot down was an Me109 fighter, and the reference to Bognor may be a deliberately obscure reference to Tangmere.

Further afield, the *Gloucester Citizen* also had the story on the Thursday. It reported:

3 Raiders destroyed

Digging was still going on last night in the wreckage of a British Restaurant in a Home Counties town...Rescuers are in the difficulty of having no check on the number of those inside when the bomb fell.[4]

After WW2, letters and features appeared in the papers at intervals, and memoirs and collections of oral history have featured air raids and precautions. These have most often discussed the People's Pantry raid, and very little has appeared about other raids. The topic is popular on Facebook and other online forums even today, with the rate of publication gathering pace into the 1990s and with the 70th anniversary. Looking at a selection of these, it is clear that accounts have fed other accounts and that various strands of the story have been created and sustained over time. These have been dealt with largely as they are relevant to this text, for example the idea that Germans were aiming for a specific building or that the bomber had been shot down. Neither occurs in a contemporary written source, yet both recur often in subsequent accounts.

In a sense, Reading has created its own memories at a popular level, so that there is a distinct set of popular accounts of the attack in 1943. This popular memory may be separate from individual memories, but may, in some instances, feed them.

Formal remembrance has taken the form of two memorials.

The first of these was erected in 1985, when what has been described as part of the west window from St Laurence's Church was placed in the church yard at the rear of the church with a simple concrete plaque, (see author's photograph overpage from 2008).

The tracery may well have been taken from the west window of the church, largely destroyed in the bombing of 1943, but research by Reading Museum suggests that this link is tenuous, and the 15th Century window may actually have been removed during renovation work in the 1860s.[5]

Early Closing Day

The second, and more prominent, memorial was unveiled on the 70th anniversary of the bombing, and is a stone set on the wall of Blandy and Blandy's solicitors, only feet way from where the fourth bomb fell on 10th February 1943.

There was discussion in the late 1990s in the local press about a plaque on the site of the Arcade, but the project behind the current memorial began in 2011 with Brian Lewendon, who as a child at school in Katesgrove, witnessed the 1943 raid.[6] Launching the campaign with the local newspapers he said

> *Many towns and cities have organised memorials for their civilians*
> *who died in air raids so I feel that Reading should not be left out.*
> *We have a great chance in 2013 to finally pay our respects and if*
> *we have that target then it gives us plenty of time. It does not need*
> *to be big or expensive, but we need something!*

An online petition was launched, but very quickly the campaign was taken up by the then Mayor, Cllr. Jenny Rynn, and a working group formed. Placing the plaque on the wall of Blandy and Blandy's put it as close to the site of two of the four bombs as possible, and on a building wrecked by the fourth SC500.

Chapter 5

There was considerable discussion about just what form the memorial plaque should take. It was decided not to include the names of those killed that day as there was insufficient information available on any who had died as a result of injuries received at some later time.[7]

The memorial was dedicated on Sunday 14th February 2013 and unveiled by two survivors of the bombing, former Mayor Brian Fowles and Derek Chamberlain – whose experiences were mentioned in Chapter 4. Over 200 people attended. In addition to Derek Chamberlain and Brian Fowles, others who had experienced the raid were present - Brian Lewendon met a friend he had not seen since his schooldays and a number of others renewed old friendships.

The Leader of the Council, Cllr. Jo Lovelock spoke of her family's experience of the raid:

My grandmother used to tell me of her terror when she,
along with many other local residents, came to the town centre
having heard of the bombing and fearing the worst for relatives and friends.

Of course, they could not get near to the scene for obvious safety reasons
and it was a long time later before she was reunited with my mother.

Although thankful for her survival the bombing had a
lasting impact; my mother never slept soundly again.[8]

Coinciding with the dedication of the memorial, Reading Museum staged an exhibition on wartime Reading, *"The Bombing of a Southern Town"*. The subject featured in a subsequent exhibition on *Reading at War*, and is described both on the Museum's website and that of the Berkshire Record Office.

Since 2013, a small annual act of remembrance had been performed at 4.30 on the 10th February at the memorial – that in 2016 actually fell on a Wednesday Newbury, bombed by a Dornier of KG40 at the same time as Reading, also dedicated a memorial to those killed.[9]

At the same time as work was underway on the memorial plaque, a proposal was made for an additional memorial.   Andrew Hood, a sculptor from Calcot proposed to use niches around St Laurence's church to hold statues representing both those killed in the raid, and the German aircrew.   Interviewed by the *Reading Chronicle* in 2012 he explained -

These people probably had nothing to do with each other until the bombing and
now we all think of them as the 41 who were killed. But the bombers are also
important because whilst they flew off and no-one thinks of them, they are an
intrinsic part of what happened on that day.[10]

Early Closing Day

So far, nothing has come of this idea.

In 2014 a proposal was made to name a new street on the site of a demolished British Gas depot - the gas works machine gunned in May 1941 - "Pantry Close" in memory of the British Restaurant. The name was part of a list put forward to the Planning Application Committee of Reading Borough Council, together with the names of local celebrities, community figures, sports people and local villages.[11] The name did not reach the shortlist.

As mentioned in the introduction, air raids have featured in the most recent generation of histories of Reading, and in 2013, a British Restaurant called the "People's Pantry" featured in Joni Pawling's autobiographical novel of her life in London, *Coal Sacks for Curtains*. The novel's Peoples Pantry was bombed at lunchtime on 10th February 1943.[12]

At the time of writing, plans for the conservation of the ruins of Reading Abbey, and development of interpretation for the area around the Abbey include both the memorial plaque and discussion of an air raid shelter dug into the remains of the Abbey's Dormitory.[13]

The site of the People's Pantry, Spring 2016.
In front of the boarded up newsagents, the alteration in the building line caused by the demolition of the arcade and People's Pantry is very evident from the corner of the building at left

(Author's photograph)

Early Closing Day

Chapter Five Notes

1. The *Reading Chronicle's* text is reproduced verbatim in Hylton (1996) pp.81 -84.

2. The *Reading Standard* covered the raid on 12th February 1943. Reading Mercury 12th may 1945 – online at http://www.arborfieldhistory.org.uk/C20/memories_bombs.htm last accessed on 11th February 2016

3. http://myweb.tiscali.co.uk/609photos/Snippets.htm last accessed on 27th February 2016

4. *Gloucester Citizen*, 11th February 1943. Accessed online on 25th February 2016

5. Brendan Carr pers. comm. to author, 7th January 2016

6. 1990s plaque – cutting from *Evening Post* dated 1997 in Drury, Colin, *Terror Raid,* Reading, 2013

7. The author was part of the working group, putting me in the somewhat odd position of being a "participant historian".

8. http://www.getreading.co.uk/news/local-news/bomb-survivor-peoples-pantry-ceremony-4192067 last accessed on 25th March 2016

9. http://www.newburyandthatchamchronicle.co.uk/news/13427221.Memories_of_Newbury_war_bombing/ last access 25th March 2016

10. http://www.readingchronicle.co.uk/news/13398454.Sculptor_plans_tribute/ Last accessed on 25th March 2016

11. http://www.reading.gov.uk/media/2381/item07/pdf/item07.pdf Last accessed on 25th March 2016

12. http://www.troubador.co.uk/book_info.asp?bookid=2438 last accessed on 25th March 2016

13. http://www.readingabbey.org.uk/fora/lesabbey/shelter.htm and http://www.readingmuseum.org.uk/get-involved/reading-abbey-quarter/reading-abbey-revealed/ last accessed 25th March 2016

Conclusion

We were just so lucky

Rosemary Siddall, Tilehurst. March 2016

Rosemary Siddall was a school girl at Kendrick School in 1943. On the 10th February she got the bus home as normal, picking it up just outside Wellsteed's in Broad Street. She lived in Gratwicke Road, Tilehurst, and had just got off the bus and was walking down Blundell's Road when her friend pointed out a plane flying very low.

I had the pleasure of a few minutes chatting to Rosemary after giving a talk about prehistoric Reading to a group meeting near my home just, as I was starting to finish off this book. Like many who witnessed the bombing in 1943, her memory is pin sharp.

On 12th June 1943 – four months after Rosemary Siddall saw the German bomber – RAF Bomber Command attacked Dusseldorf, now one of Reading's twin towns.

In under half an hour, starting at twenty five past one in the morning, around 600 Halifaxes and Lancasters dropped over 200,000 four pound incendiary bombs and upwards of 1,300 high explosive bombs on the city, killing 600 people and injuring around 3000.[1] A raid the following April killed around twice the number lost on June 12th 1943.

A post war Allied survey found that 130% of Dusseldorf's buildings had been damaged by air attack. In other words, every building had been damaged, some repaired and then damaged again.[2] In all, Dusseldorf was bombed ten times by the Allies, taking over 18,000 tons of bombs and losing 64% of the buildings in the Allies' target area – representing an acreage greater than that of central Reading.[3] At least six German cities received a greater tonnage of bombs, and thirteen saw a greater percentage of the "target" destroyed.

In 1945 a visiting United States Army Air Force officer found Dusseldorf "not even a ghost".[4]

Looking at the historical picture surveyed here, Reading did not experience the fate of Dusseldorf because -

Early Closing Day

    a. It lacked the industrial base to make it a worthwhile target

    b. It lacked a feature of any real strategic significance – for example a port

    c. For most of the war the main Luftwaffe bombing effort was against the Soviet Union

    d. The Luftwaffe was not equipped for a strategic bombing campaign at all,

    e. In 1940-41 when a sustained effort was made to bomb Britain, whilst it could put hundreds of bombers over a target in one night, the Luftwaffe lacked the ability to lift the tonnage of bombs needed to achieve such destruction

Sitting on a grey October morning in the back bedroom of our cosy home in Tilehurst, I know that in 1943 our nearest public air raid shelter would have been in Newbery Park – I played on its concreted up remains as a child. Our nearest ARP wardens were based at post B4, which was finally removed in the 1970s. Although the names of the wardens have not survived, their Head Warden, Mr. Hedges, lived in School Road, just round the corner. For first aid we could have gone to the Laurels, now part of Park Lane School, and next to Tilehurst Library where both my wife and I have worked, and where I used to sit whilst my father took forever to choose his books on Saturdays. Corporation run repair and rescue parties were within about half a mile of us, and information and advice after a raid would have been available just up the road. Warning would have come from a siren on the Water Tower, which, until new house building, I could see from the window of this room.

This is a highly subjective reaction, from someone who was born and grew up in Reading, but it is clear that the provision made for dealing with bombing in Reading reached to a very local level, and featured intimately in people's lives. This, perhaps more than the actual results of bombs being dropped, seems to be the real impact of air raids on Reading.

Chapter 1 of this book showed that the perception of the possibilities of air attack was never matched by the reality (even in UK targets badly hit). It shows the scale of Reading's preparations for air attack, but also its intimacy. Although a single Halifax or Lancaster could have dropped all the bombs dropped on Reading by the Luftwaffe, the bombs that fell still killed people and wrecked people's homes. Earlier this year (2015) I had a routine business meeting in a school machine gunned in 1943, and I've talked about bombing to audiences in a library hit by incendiaries in 1940. Yet, looking at air raids on Reading shows that regardless of the physical damage done, the perceived and real threats of air attack made the Second World War something that happened at a very local level for the town's inhabitants due in great part to the depth and scale of civil defence..

There was a direct cost to the town even if no bombs had fallen. Whilst central government paid up to 60% of the cost of civil defence, thousands of pounds had to be contributed by the Corporation, and this, together with staff-hours can only have had an opportunity cost in terms of projects not completed or undertaken. Given the materials used here, it is not possible to suggest at any level other than speculation whether civil defence had any impact on, for example, provision of housing by the Corporation, but it will have had a day to day impact on its operations. In December 1942 the Housing Committee stated that repairs to war damaged buildings had cost £3000, and later recorded explicitly the enforced stoppage of housing work.

In 1939, the total wage bill for civil defence for one week was £1849. Using inflation in retail prices as a measure, this would give £90,170 in 2016 money.[5] If wage inflation is used, it gives £249,900 - wages have risen more than prices, particularly post World War Two. Taking this as a representative figure – and numbers rose towards 1942, and were scaled down in 1944-45 – the wage cost to Reading of Civil Defence from 1939-44 (when dismantlement of provision began) may have been around £50 million at today's prices.

At a given point all that amount would have had to be spent by the Corporation, but, as mentioned, at least 60% would have been met by grant funding from central government claimed afterwards. However, whilst it's hard to see that such expenditure didn't stop the Corporation from doing other things, it may not be true that 1939-45 need necessarily have shown its effects completely on the debit side for the town. Housing development may have been held back, and Corporation income from rates lost due to the demolition of some buildings – as in 1943.

Although lives and injury cannot be costed in these terms, the financial cost to the town needs to be seen in the light of the effects of the war as a whole.

Early Closing Day

Many people did long unpaid hours in the Fire Guard, but throughout the war wages rose, and there was virtually full employment. Building firms complained to the Corporation of the effects of men and vehicles used for civil defence, yet benefitted from spending on air raid shelters (and indeed on repairs to bomb damage). Civil defence jobs were real jobs, and put money into the local economy. Food prices were being managed nationally, and, for example, the People's Pantry, with part of its dual role linked explicitly to bombing, played a part in supporting people to eat better for less.

Chapter 2 shows that although never severe, German bombing in the main period of attack reached across the town, stepping precaution up to reality for families and those in the ARP services. Reading was actually hit a very few times, but alerts are recorded and remembered as regular features of life, at least in 1940-41. By 1943, Reading's inhabitants had given up bothering to take air raid sirens seriously, but for a period in 1940-41 they had taken to sleeping in their Andersons and in street and trench shelters. They stayed awake at night fire watching or as part of the wardens service, and volunteered to give out food and make bandages. When, in the space of moments, four bombs killed 41 people on a Wednesday in 1943, Chapter 3 shows that the resources put in place by the Civil Defence and Emergency Committee, and other organisations could respond effectively, dealing with at least the immediate effects.

Chapters 2, 3 and 4 also illustrate that Reading's preparedness for bombing did not mean that it had to rely solely on its own resources. The town was a part of a bigger picture and able to call on the resources of its ARP Region when needed, but also of the military, both British and United States based locally.

Similarly, as Chapter 3 shows, Reading was not the sole focus of Luftwaffe attack on that early closing day in 1943. Just as civil defence in the town was part of a regional and national picture, so the attack launched upon it was part of a strategy for attacks on the UK that formed part of an overall strategic position. Reading was a target in an operation covering much of the South East delivered by a German command structure with an area of operations ranging from Toulouse and Bordeaux in the south west to the north of Holland. The attack on Reading was part of a "front" covering the main Atlantic coastline of German occupied Europe.

Conclusion

Despite many suggestions, the only contemporary evidence to suggest why the town was bombed that day points to -

a. A General policy of nuisance/terror bombing in the west on the part of the German Air Force at that time

b. A number of raids launched across the South East that afternoon, hitting towns of no particular strategic value in themselves

c. That the lone bomber may have been aiming for the railway, a target present on the only two contemporary German intelligence sources known at the time of writing, one which was visible and findable. The parallel with the attack on Newbury, where the railway may also have been the target, is striking. However, although a contemporary view from a source tasked to take an informed judgement, this may be a rationalisation, and the Dornier's crew may simply have been looking to bomb the approximate centre of the town.

Chapter 4 shows that whilst physical damage to people and buildings took time to heal – if it ever did – the actual incident of 10th February 1943 was contained and dealt with quickly. The siting of the main daytime control centre in the centre of town can appear to have been an error, and clearly its own defences against attack were insufficient, but around it there was sufficient resilience to make a coordinated response possible and effective. Despite the loss of life, nothing of direct importance to the war effort was hit and the resources consumed were largely those put aside for the purpose.

It was the provision of those resources, the organisation and sheer work involved alongside the awareness of the possibility of attack that shaped Reading's wartime experience of air raids.

Early Closing Day

Conclusion Notes

1. https://de.wikipedia.org/wiki/Luftangriffe_auf_D%C3%BCsseldorf accessed on 18th October 2015
2. Richard Overy. *Bombing war*. (Penguin, 2014) pp.470
3. Max Hastings. *Bomber Command* (Pan, 1979) pp.446.
4. Overy, op.cit. pp.410
5. My thanks go to Neil Grant for wrangling the figures and good advice on this point.

Bibliography

Primary sources and other sources used for specific points are referred to in references with each chapter.

With the exception of Stuart Hylton's work, there is no overall history of Reading in WW2, and so the books given here are mainly general introductions to the "Home Front" in the Second World War used as contextual support. Stuart's *Reporting the Blitz* (History Press, 2012) covers more than Reading, but has useful material from the Reading papers for 1940-41.

Reading

Stuart Hylton. *A History of Reading*. Chichester: Phillimore, 1997

Stuart Hylton. *Reading at war*. Stroud: Alan Sutton Publishing, 1996

Daphne Phillips. *The Story of Reading.* Revised Edition. Newbury: Countryside Books, 1990

Civil Defence

Martin Brayley. *The British Home Front 1939-45.* Oxford: Osprey Publishing, 2005 (Elite 109)

Mike Brown. *Put that light out: Britain's Civil Defence services at war 1939-1945*. Stroud: Sutton Publishing, 1999

Tim Essex-Lopresti (Ed.) *A Brief history of Civil Defence.* Matlock: Civil Defence Association, 2005. Available online at http://www.civildefenceassociation.org.uk/ histcdweba4v7.pdf

Home Front

Basil Collier. *The Defence of the United Kingdom*. London: HMSO, 1957

Lizzie Cottingham. *The Taste of war*. London: Penguin, 2012

Juliet Gardiner. *The Blitz*. London: Harper Press, 2010

Juliet Gardiner. *Wartime Britain 1939-1945*. London: Headline Book Publishing, 2004.

S.P Mackenzie. The *Home Guard: A political and military history*. Oxford: Oxford University Press, 1995

Richard Overy. *The Bombing War: Europe 1939-1945*. London: Penguin, 2014

Alfred Price. *Britain's air defences 1939-45*. Oxford: Osprey Publishing, 2004 (Elite 104)

Early Closing Day

According to the captioning in Reading Museum's collection of images from the *Berkshire Chronicle*, this tabby cat – whose name is not know – was rescued from the roof of the People's Pantry after the attack.
Reading Museum REDMG : 1980.36.A570.7.
Copyright Reading Museum (Reading Borough Council. All rights reserved.

Appendix 1

List of those killed or died of injuries Wednesday 10th February 1943

Surname	Forenames	Title	Age	Location	Home address	Other details
Barnes	Ernest Cheeseman	Mr	64	Market St	32 Carey St	Commonwealth War Graves Commission (CWGC) has 67
Beswick	Ernest Morley	Mr	32	Peoples Pantry	Beech Rd Purley	
Brown	Violet May	Miss	10	Minster St	7 Smalls Court, London St	Daughter of Gen. James Edward Brown and Ethel Brown
Byland	Catherine Elizabeth	Miss	47	Arcade	1007 Oxford Rd	Daughter of Elizabeth May and the late John
Chandler	Florence Alice	Mrs	64	Peoples Pantry	6 Seaton Gardens Whitley Estate	Widow of Thomas Henry Chandler
Costin	Jesse	Ms?	73	Peoples Pantry	148 Great Knollys St	
Crook	Dennis Roy	Mr	18	Town Hall	5 Spring Gardens	Son of Ivy May Crook
Dixon	Nellie	Miss	28	Peoples Pantry		Daughter of James and Mary Dixon, 6 Thomas St. Gorey, Co. Wexford, Irish Republic
Doran	James Herbert	Mr	62	Cheddar Cheese, Broad St	3 Greyfriars Rd	Killed In yard outside Cheddar Cheese
Dowling	Arthur John	Mr	61	Town Hall (Outside)	158 Great Knollys St	
Eaton	Edward Augustus	Warden	58	Market Place	46 Wilton Crescent Southampton	Warden for Southampton County Borough; husband of Lydia Clara Eaton
Godden	Henry	Mr	61	Friar Street	3 Holybrook Rd	Husband of May Godden
Harding	Edward George	Mr	58	29 Market Place . Arthur Cooper Wine Merchants	3 Greyfriars Rd	
Hickey	William Ernest	Mr	69	Peoples Pantry	133 Gosbrook Rd	Son of late William and Ellen Hickey
Hobbs	Ernest Gilbert	Mr	69	Peoples Pantry	29 Argyle St	
Hooban	William Patrick	Mr	61	Arcade	11 Salcombe Drive	Husband of Annie Ellen Hooban

Early Closing Day

Surname	Forenames	Title	Age	Location	Home address	Other details
Humphrys	Edward Joseph	Mr	33	Peoples Pantry	3 Hampton Cottages, New Rd Bracknell	Husband of Jean Winifred Humphrys
Jupp	Rex	PC	24	29 Market Place . Arthur Cooper Wine Merchants	17 Ennerdale Road	Killed by enemy action while on patrol during an enemy air raid http//www.policememorial.org.uk/ Forces/Thames_Valley /Thames_Valley_Roll.htm
Kersley	Reginald Martin Deane	Mr	58	Market Place	13 Stanhope Rd	Husband of E.N Kerseley
Macrini/ Maccarini	Aristide	Mr	63	29 Market Place. Arthur Cooper Wine Merchants	86 London St	Master of Philosophy, Italian national. Husband of late Carla Macrini. Daughter ambulance driver at Castle Depot Commended (BRO DEX 1657/2)
Merchant	Arthur James	Mr	56	Peoples Pantry	2 Sherman Place	
Miles	Julia	Mrs ?	69	Peoples Pantry	215 Barkham Rd. Wokingham	
Osborne	Edith Rosa	Mrs	49	Peoples Pantry	168 Southampton St	Daughter of late Harry and Louisa Banwell. Wife of Leading Seaman Victor Osborne
Parker	Emily Evelyn	Miss	25	Peoples Pantry	169 Southampton St	CWGC has age as 30. Mr Cave of 51a 168 Southampton Street reported Miss Parker and Mrs Osbourne had gone to the Peoples Pantry at 16.15. Mr Cave identified Miss Parker at CWS mortuary on 11th Feb (BRO DEX 1657/2)
Parsons	Betty	Miss	11	Minster St	10 The Grove off South St	CWGC says 12. Daughter of Charles James Parson
Pateman	Dorothy	Mrs	36	Peoples Pantry		WVS volunteer - Daughter of William Storm Jameson and Hannah Margaret Jameson of Ryedale, Whitby, Yorks. Wife of Cyril Robert Joseph Pateman.
Pike	Mildred Florence	Mrs	29	29 Market Place . Arthur Cooper Wine Merchants	35 Tilehurst Rd	Daughter of Harriet and late Albert Stone of The Redoubt, New Rd Clanfield, Portsmouth. Widow of Albert Charles Pike

Appendices

Surname	Forenames	Title	Age	Location	Home address	Other details
Sayer	Arthur	Mr	65	Peoples Pantry	5 Baker St	
Seymour	Frank	Mr	49	1 Friar St	101 Hamilton Rd	Son of Albert Cole and Ellen Seymour of 54 Westgate St Gloucester. Husband of Laura
Simmonds	Ellen	Mrs	75	Peoples Pantry	8 St Giles Buildings	Widow of George
Smith	Arthur James	Mr	60		Aldershot	CWGC says 65
Temple	William Henry James	Mr	58	Town Hall (Outside)	84 Kings Rd Caversham	Husband of Maud May Temple
Thompson	Ellen Anne	Mrs	51	Peoples Pantry	114 Linden Rd Shinfield Estate	Daughter of John and Emily Vesty, School Lane, Quorn, Liecs. Widow of Horace John Thompson
Wilmott	John	Mr	72	Peoples Pantry	22 Silver St	Identified by son 11th Feb. ARP gave address as 23 Silver St
Langford	George Albert		10	Peoples Pantry	3 Salcombe Rd, Whitley	Son of Albert and Elsie Langford. Died Battle Hospital 11th Feb
Thackeray	Margaret Joan	Miss	29	Town Hall	13 Brooklyn Drive, Emmer Green	Daughter of Robert Reavely Thackeray and Elizabeth Margaret Thackeray, of 13 Brooklyn Drive, Emmer Green. Injured 10 February 1943, at Municipal Buildings; died at Royal Berks Hospital (RBH)
Weinstein	Lily	Mrs	46		41 Baker St	Wife of Pte Goodie Weinstein RAMC. Died RBH 16 Feb

Early Closing Day

Appendix 2

Transcript of *Berkshire Chronicle's* list of those injured and taken to hospital, Wednesday 10th February 1943

Surname	First Name/Title	Notes
Anderson	William	Aged 41
Griffin	Stanley	Aged 49
Thomas	Mrs Alfred	
Kelly	Kathleen	
Blandy	Mr	
Woodley	Mrs	
Ashworth or Ashwell	Mrs	
Child ?	Charles ?	
Clerk ?	Oliver?	
Luffman or Lusman	Mrs	
Buckley	Muriel Ruth?	
Day	Joan E?	
Dore	Dorothy	
Gallagher	Katherine	
Parlow or Barlow		
Watkins	Muriel	
Yarley	Anthony	
Ingram?	Frances	
Townsend	Harold	
Weston	Frederick G	
Keading or Reading	William	
Miles - child of Mrs (name not known)		
Litcombe?	Miss	
Chamberlain	Derek	Peoples Pantry
Batchelor	Mrs	
Abery	Charlotte	
Tulles?	Hugh	
Pelsher ?	Percy	
Butler	Annie	
Gale	William	
Padwick	Ann	
Parsons	Ivy	Minster St.
Sturgess	Arthur	

Appendices

Surname	First Name/Title	Notes
Knicker (actually Nicker)	Cecilia	Peoples Pantry
Cope	Evan	
Kennedy	?	
Brown	Clarence	Minster St
Barnes	Mrs Rosa	
Hutchins	Mr	
Townsend	Mr	

Early Closing Day

Appendix 3

ARP Wardens' posts in 1940

Headquarters: Market Passage, Reading

Chief Warden: Ronald S Ruston. "Suffolk House" 9 Liebenrood Rd. Reading

Deputy Chief Wardens

M.M. Williams "Windygates", 36 Shinfield Rd, Reading

Insp. W.J. Seager, 86 Grange Avenue

F.B. Gleave, 256 Tilehurst Rd

A Finn Ramsbury Drive, Earley

Group A – 12 Posts, 31 Sectors

Headquarters: Old Grove House, Surley Row Caversham

Head Warden 1940: T.J.Hubbard, 17 Brooklyn Drive, Emmer Green

Group B – 8 Posts, 21 Sectors

Headquarters: Triangle, School Rd, Tilehurst

Head Warden: H.L.Hedges, 78 School Rd, Tilehurst

Group C – 9 Posts, 25 Sectors

Headquarters: 19 Parkside Rd, Reading

Head Warden: J.W.H. Perrin, 19 Parkside Rd, Reading

Group D – 5 Posts, 11 Sectors

Headquarters: Basement, ARP Offices, Market Passage, Market Place, Reading

Head Warden: H.E. Hollay, 161 Friar St, Reading

Group E – 6 Posts, 21 Sectors

Headquarters: Simonds' Brewery

Head Warden: A.G. Negus, 40 Franklin St, Reading

Group F - 5 Posts, 22 Sectors

Headquarters: 102 Kendrick Rd, Reading

Head Warden: B.L.R Dowse, 102 Kendrick Rd, Reading

Appendices

Group G – 8 Posts, 28 Sectors

Headquarters: Library, Northumberland Avenue

Head Warden; Capt. W.E.M. Blandy, 12 Christchurch Gardens, Reading

Group H – 6 Posts, 23 Sectors

Headquarters: 7 Erleigh Rd, Reading

Head Warden: A.H. Wintle, 7 Erleigh Rd, Reading

Group I – 5 Posts, 23 Sectors

Headquarters: Basement, Alfred Sutton School, Crescent Rd, Reading

Head Warden: C.T.M. Weekes, 13 Whiteknights Rd, Reading

Early Closing Day

ARP Warden posts c.1940

Post number	1940 List in Pocket Guide to Air Raid Precautions [1]	Map [2]	Notes
A1	EL Substation, Gosbrook Rd. Caversham	N side between St John's Rd and Bryant Ave	
A2	Caversham Parochial School, School Lane	E side	
A3	EL Substation in Hemdean Rd	E side opposite Victoria Rd	
A4	No2 Kidmore Rd		
A5	Darell Rd	E side near junction with St Peter's Hill	
A6	Green Hill, The Warren	N side	
A7	West Dene, Upper Woodcote Rd	Post opposite end St Peter's Ave	

A8	171 Kidmore Rd	S side of Road near Uplands Rd	
A9	Old Grove House, Surley Row	Opposite end St Barnabas	Group A Headquarters
A10	Peppard Rd, near Surley Row	? W side near junction	
A11	EL Substation, Chiltern Rd	? Corner Grosvenor Rd	
A12	Holloway's Garage, Henley Rd	? N side near junction with	
B1	Middle of roundabout near Tilehurst Station	Opposite end Rodway Rd	Not extant 2008
B2	Junction Weald Rise and Thirlmere Ave	E side of road	Built over post war?
B3	Garage at the Bell, Oxford Rd	N Side of road	
B4	Armour Hill	N side W of junction with Lwr Armour Rd	"Air Raid Shelter" in Newbery Park (area known as Sheepwash?)
B5	Highways Depot, Norcot Rd	Post shown S of road near	
B6	Triangle	Shown on Triangle itself	Group B Headquarters. Underground shelter extant into 1970s

B7	EL Substation, City Rd	N side near junction with Park Lane	Shelter or post extant in grounds of nursery school in Recreation Rd, 2008
B8	In front of Church, Church Rd	Shown on E side	Extant 2008
C1	Battle Farm, Beresford Rd Entrance		
C2	Basement Battle School, Cranbury Rd Entrance		Possible half-underground structure now in use as heating plant
C3	Rear of Library, Oxford Rd	N side of Oxford Rd opposite end Kensington Rd	No freestanding structure extant 2008, but library manager reports older customers recall a post or shelter
C4	640 Oxford Rd	N side of Oxford Rd just E of Beecham Rd	
C5	Grovelands School, Junction Oxford Rd/ Constitution Rd	Shown on triangle of land	Post or shelter on Grovelands/ Oxford Rd junction extant into 1980s and in use as lavatory.
C6	Prospect Park near Water Rd	S side of Tilehurst Rd, just E of Water Rd	Extant 2008, closed public lavatory, demolished 2009
C7	Opposite junction Bath Rd and Burghfield Rd	N side of Bath Rd opposite Burghfield Rd	
C8	Junction Monks Way, Southcote Lane	Shown at Junction	
C9	Wilton House, Westcote Rd	S side of Westcote at junction with Parkside Rd	

Early Closing Day

G3	Dug-out in grounds of Clinic Northumberland Avenue	? W side E of Dawlish Rd	
G4	Whitley Park School, Brixham Rd Entrance	W side of Brixham Rd	
G5	Dug-out Merton Rd	E side of Merton Rd, half way between Stockton Rd and Callington Rd	
G6	Lower Whitley School, Whitley Wood Lane	? E side Basingstoke Rd	
G7	Junction Linden Rd and Hazel Crescent	W side at Junction	
G8	Dug-out Leighton Park School, North Lodge, Shinfield Rd	E of Northumberland Rd, N of junction with Cressingham Rd	
H1	Junction of Watlington St and Queens Rd	Possibly on E side of Watlington St	
H2	Fisherman's Cottage PH entrance, Orts Rd	N side Orts Rd	
H3	West Lodge, Victoria Square, King's Rd	W side of Square at junction with King's Rd	
H4	Rear of St Luke's Hall		
H5	St. Joseph's Convent, Lydford Rd	N side of Lydford Rd	
H6	Craven Rd, entrance to Reading School	E side Craven Rd towards Addington Rd	
?		N side of Erleigh Rd, between Alexandra and Donnington Rds	
I1	59a Cholmeley Rd	W side opposite Coventry Rd	
I2	London Rd entrance to Palmer Park	E of St Bartholomew's Rd	
I3	Wokingham Rd entrance to Palmer Park	Not shown	
I4	Basement, Alfred Sutton School, Crescent Rd entrance	S of side of Crescent Rd, W of Wokingham Rd	
I5	Holmes Rd	N side of Road	

Appendices

Appendix 4

Civil Defence employees 1940-42

Number employed at 26 July 1940   From: National Archives HO186/275

War Establishment of No 6 Region – Reading

	Male	Female	Total
Wardens	984	246	1230
35 First Aid Parties	165		165
Personnel for First Aid Parties	40	200	240
Drivers for 50 ambulances		200	200
Drivers for 35 cars		66	66
13 Light Rescue Parties	84		84
3 Heavy Rescue Parties	27		27
9 Decontamination Squads	63		63
Report Centre	12	36	48
Messengers	30		30
Total	**216**	**36**	**2153**

BRO R/AC2/20/A – Reading Corporation Emergency Committee Minutes

Early Closing Day

Statement of wages paid in ARP services weeks ending 22 and 29 September 1939

Service	Week ending 22 Sept (£)	Week ending 29 Sept
Air Raid Wardens	709	693
Auxiliary Firemen	291	287
First Aid Posts	156	287
Control Room	27	33
Siren operators	11	8
Ambulance Drivers	111	111
Rescue and demolition parties	242	237
Road and Demolition parties	131	128
First Police Reserve	55	55
Police War Reserve	116	151
Total	1849	1990

Meeting of 27 October 1941

	Unit Establishment	Personell	Second Line
Wardens	630	1375	50
First Aid Parties	174	219	
Decontamination	63	63	
Rescue	155	155	
Report and Control	35	210	100
Gas Identification	6	6	
Total	1063	2028	159

2 July 1942

Appendices

	Unit Establishment	Personell	Part Time
Wardens	630	1890	700
First Aid Parties	174	522	400
Decontamination	63	189	150
Rescue	155	310	200
Report and Control	35	210	50
Messengers	63	245	
Total	1120	3366	1500

Early Closing Day

Appendix 5

Air Raid Sirens in Reading

From minutes of the Civil Defence Committee meeting of 24 Jan 1940

Town Hall

Fire Station

Highways yard, Emmer Green

Highways yard, Gosbrook Rd

Messers Collier, Grovelands

CWS Preserve Works, Coley

H&G Simmonds, Bridge St

Wantage Hall

Tilehurst Water Tower

Home Office Regional Store

CWS Printing Works, Elgar Rd

CWS bakery Grovelands

Gasworks

Co-op Cemetery Junction

Additional sirens approved 3rd Oct 1940

Highmoor Road

Kentwood Hill – moved to Tilehurst Potteries 30 Oct

Oxford Rd

Appendices

Appendix 6

Numbers of air raid shelters in Reading

	11 Dec 1939	Report for Dec 1939	22 Jan 1940	Report Feb 1940	29 July 1940	Report 26th September 1940
Anderson Shelters						4155 delivered, 4100 erected – places for 15,400 people
Morrison Shelters						
Domestic Surface						3000 = 11426 people
Domestic Basement						
Public						
School						
Total Places	7400 completed with 2500 approved	8700	4550 always open; 5405 open 9am-11pm, 8746 open during business hours	9059 including trenches	11,120	

Early Closing Day

	Report 22 Oct 1940	Report 31 Oct 1940	Report 3 Dec 1940	Report 29th Jan 1941	Report 4th March 1941	Report April 1941	Report May 1941
Anderson Shelters	4145 erected		4145	4305 delivered, places for 15400 people	4709 delivered, places for 15700 people	5350 delivered plus 336 extensions. Spaces for 20,400 people	5987 + 540 extensions delivered
Morrison Shelters							
Domestic Surface	3900 = 14851 people plus 700 building /2667 people		5100 homes = 19400 people plus 1010/3850 places building	6660 homes, 942 building. 25367 plus 3579 building	7400 households with 760 building. Places for 28120 people with 2879 building	7880 homes, spaces for 29950. 656 homes have shelter building, places for 2471 people	8850 homes served, 405 building. Places for 33,652 plus 1571 building
Domestic Basement	2 – 124 people			3 shelters with 125 places	3 shelters with 125 places	3 shelters with 125 places	3 shelters with 125 places
Public	11,597 people plus 820 places building		12314 places plus 450 building	12987 places, 210 building	13117 places with 760 building	13317 places with 1360 building	13467 plus 1260 places building
School	11,700 people plus 400 building		11900 places plus 300 building	12,600 places with 300 building	12,600 places with 200 building	12800 places	12800 places with 200 building
Total Places		11984 places in public shelters		66479		76592	

Appendices

	Report June 1941	Report July 1941	21st July 1941
Anderson Shelters	6580 + 621 extensions delivered. Places for 25000 people	6955 with 1229 extensions delivered. Places for 26,400 people	4141 in first allotment. 2800 in second. 45 collected and redelivered. 467 erected by Corporation. 2350 extensions received, 1368 delivered, 483 made by highways
Morrison Shelters			750 received. 250 delivered free, 26 paid for. 2 collected and redelivered.
Domestic Surface	9410 houses served with 188 building. Places for 35728 with 715 building	9920 households with 182 building	
Domestic Basement	4 shelters with 149 places	4 shelters with 149 places	
Public	15790 places with 960 building	14490 places with 1210 building	
School	13000 places	13000	
Total Places	87667	91729	

Early Closing Day

Appendix 7

Locations suffering air attack 1940-44.

Note: "Area" is an approximate one only, rather than a reference to a specific Ward

Street	Area	Date
Albert Rd	Caversham	10/02/1943
Anglefield Rd	Caversham	01/10/1940
Baker St	Reading	09/04/1941
Bartletts Place	Reading	09/04/1941
Basingstoke Rd	Reading	09/04/1941
Beech Lane	Earley	19/06/1944
Berkeley Avenue	Coley	03/10/1940
Boston Ave	Coley	09/04/1941
Broad St	Reading	10/02/1943
Brunswick St	Reading	09/04/1940
Buckside	Caversham	26/11/1940
Bulmershe Woods	Earley	12/10/1940
Butts Hill Rd	Woodley	30/01/1941
Cardiff Rd	Reading	26/11/1940
Castle Crescent	Coley	03/10/1940
		09/04/1941
Castle Lodge	Coley	09/04/1941
Chester St	Caversham	26/11/1940
Chiltern Rd	Caversham	01/10/1940
Church Rd	Caversham	30/01/1941
Church St	Caversham	26/11/1940
		30/01/1941
Clifton Park Rd	Caversham	30/01/1941
Coley Ave	Coley	09/04/1941
Coley Park Farm	Coley	15/11/1940
Coley Recreation Ground	Coley	09/04/1941
Crockhamwell Lane	Woodley	22/06/1942
Cromwell Rd	Caversham	30/01/1941
Dover St	Coley	03/10/1940

Appendices

Street	Area	Date
Elm Rd	Earley	19/06/1944
Erlegh Court Gardens	Earley	30/09/1940
Ford Lane	Woodley	22/06/1942
Friar St	Reading	10/02/1943
Hemdean Rd	Caversham	26/11/1940
		30/01/1941
		10/02/1943
Hemdean Rise	Caversham	30/01/1941
Henley Rd	Caversham	30/01/1941
House Close	Caversham	26/11/1940
Kidmore End Rd	Caversham	09/10/1940
Kings Rd (gasworks)	Reading	12/05/1941
		12/09/1940
		10/05/1941
Langley Hill	Tilehurst	05/11/1940
Littlecote Drive	Reading	09/04/1941
Lower Henley Rd	Caversham	01/10/1940
		30/01/1941
Mansfield Rd	Reading	09/04/1941
Meadow Rd	Caversham	26/11/1940
Ministry of Health	Coley	09/04/1941
Minster St	Reading	10/02/1943
Newlands Ave	Caversham	26/11/1940
North Lake	Woodley	22/06/1942
North St	Caversham	30/01/1941
Oratory School	Caversham	01/10/1940
		26/11/1940
Oxford Rd	Tilehurst	10/02/1943
Oxford St	Caversham	26/11/1940
Pembroke Place	Caversham	01/10/1940
Peppard Rd	Caversham	09/10/1940
		26/11/1940

Early Closing Day

Street	Area	Date
Priory Ave	Caversham	30/01/1941
Prospect St	Caversham	30/01/1941
Rectory Rd	Caversham	30/01/1941
Salisbury Rd	Reading	26/11/1940
Short St	Caversham	30/01/1941
South Lake	Woodley	12/09/1940
South St	Caversham	26/11/1940
South View Avenue	Caversham	30/01/1941
St Annes Rd	Caversham	30/01/1941
St Laurences Church	Reading	10/02/1943
St Peters Ave	Caversham	30/01/1941
St Peters Church	Caversham	30/01/1941
St Saviours Rd	Coley	03/10/1940
Star Rd	Caversham	01/10/1940
		30/01/1941
Stone St	Reading	10/02/1943
Suttons Trial Grounds	Earley	30/09/1940
		10/05/1941
Tilehurst Rd	Reading	09/04/1941
Town Hall	Reading	10/02/1943
Upper Henley Rd	Caversham	01/10/1940
Westfield Rd	Caversham	30/01/1941
Westwood Row	Tilehurst	19/11/1940
Wolesley St	Coley	03/10/1940
Woodley Airfield	Woodley	16/08/1940
		16/09/1940
		03/10/1940

Notes to Appendices

1. Pocket Guide to the ARP Arrangements in Reading op.cit and Committee minutes at BRO R/AC2/20/1a
2. Laminated map in artefact box collection, Reading Museum. Date uncertain

Index

Early Closing Day

Index

Early Closing Day

Whitley : 9, 16 ,18, 30 ,37, 40 ,43, 45, 101, 103, 108, 116, 121, 122, 135, 157, 159, 166
Wokingham: 36, 40 ,46, 75, 76, 121, 124, 158, 166
Women's Voluntary Service: 43, 47, 48, 54, 98, 101, 103, 112, 116, 117, 118, 125, 139, 158
Woodley: 3, 4, 7, 9, 10 ,11, 17, 36,57,59,75, 76, 77, 78,90, 160, 174, 175, 176
WVS – SEE Women's Voluntary Service
Z (Rocket Battery SEE Anti Aircraft Defence)

The Author

Mike Cooper has had a lifelong interest in history, especially military and local history. Following a history degree at the University of Reading he worked as a librarian, with both the University and Reading Library. In addition to work on librarianship, he has had two previous books on the history of Reading published – *We Cannot Park on Both Sides* (1999) dealing with Reading volunteers in the Spanish Civil War, and *A Hamlet Called Harmour* (2001) about the Armour Road area of Tilehurst. He has written booklets for Reading Libraries on the history of Tilehurst and Southcote. Mike's talks on local history topics to audiences including the History of Reading Society have included prehistoric Reading, the Battle of Maiwand and food in wartime.

The author speaking at a WEA workshop on wartime Reading in 2013.

Scallop Shell Press

Who we are

Ever since the Middle Ages the scallop shell has been the symbol of those
going on pilgrimage to the shrine of St James in Compostela, Spain.

Today the pilgrimage is even more popular than ever as people of all faiths, and none,
seek a meaning for their journey through life.

The shell became a metaphor for the journey, the grooves representing
the many ways of arriving at one's destination.
At a practical level the shell was also useful for scooping up water to drink or food to eat.

We, at Scallop Shell Press, aim to publish works which, like the grooves of the shell, will
offer the modern pilgrim stories of our shared humanity and help readers arrive at their
own meaningful interpretations of life. We hope that our books will be shells within
whose covers readers will find an intellectual and spiritual source of sustenance for their
own personal pilgrimages.

John and Lindsay Mullaney

Some other published titles

Reformation, Revolution and Rebirth,   John Mullaney and Lindsay Mullaney

Catholic Reading, A Pilgrimage Trail, edited by J and L Mullaney

The Cowslade Manuscript, edited by Lindsay Mullaney

The Longuet Papers, edited by Lindsay Mullaney

The Stained Glass of St James' Church Reading, John Mullaney

The Timms Family of Reading and London, Katie Amos

The Mansion House, Katie Amos

Reading's Abbey Quarter. An Illustrated History, John Mullaney

The Reading Abbey Stone, John Mullaney

If you would like to find out more about Scallop Shell Press visit our website

Scallopshellpress.co.uk